ARGONAUT LIBRARY OF ANTIQUITIES

THE TWO AGORAS IN ANCIENT ATHENS

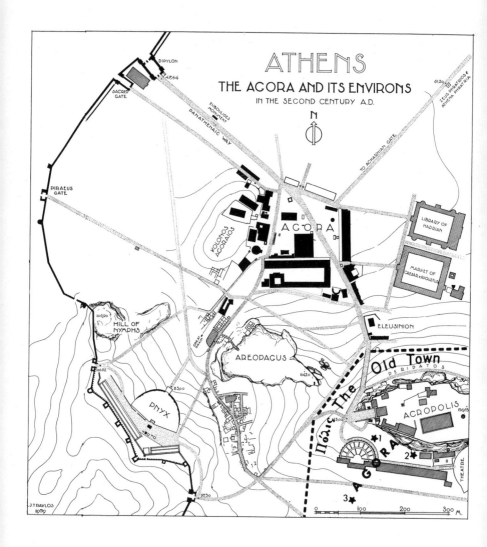

ATHENS

THE AGORA AND ITS ENVIRONS
IN THE SECOND CENTURY A.D.

Until the year 479 BC, when the Persians destroyed the city of Athens by fire, the Agora or market-place of the city was located at the entrance to the Acropolis in the area enclosed by the Pelargikon ring wall (indicated by a broken line). The triangle formed by the numbers 1, 2 and 3 was its natural location. When a new city was rebuilt from the ruins, the Agora was transferred to the area below the Kolonos Hill. Three main landmarks remain to prove the existence and location of the earlier forgotten Agora of the Old Town. 1. The Temple of Aphrodite Pandemos, 2. The First Enneakrounos, and 3. The Sanctuary of Nymphe. Ancient authors and inscriptions supply the remaining information to support the distinction between THE TWO AGORAS IN ANCIENT ATHENS.

THE TWO AGORAS
IN
ANCIENT ATHENS

A New Commentary on
Their History and Development
Topography and Monuments

by

Al. N. Oikonomides

Research Director, Argonaut
Library of Antiquities

ARGONAUT, INC., PUBLISHERS
CHICAGO   MCMLXIV

Library of Congress Catalogue Card Number: LC 64-23440

CONTENTS

PREFACE

Now that the main part of my research on the testimonia in ancient texts related to the topography of my beloved native city Athens is printed in its final form, and now that the neglected testimonia of early Athenian religion and topography, unknown to many fellow scholars, are set forth both in Greek in English, together with the necessary commentary and notes, as an Athenian first and an archaeologist second, I have the feeling of a soldier who has done what he could in his own area of the battlefield, in this case in the battle to regain lost historical knowledge and to restore the truth amidst some misguided beliefs.

Several years have passed since the first notes of this research project were put into a separate file. In my papers filled with original manuscripts the first pages have the heading of the Acropolis Museum and others are in notebooks from the University of Athens and the Agora Museum in the Stoa of Attalos. There are also notes on stationery of the 3rd Division of the Greek Cavalry and the Division of the Royal Mounted Guards, and jottings from the Louvre and the library of the British Museum. And finally there are the notes from the Metropolitan Museum of New York and those produced more recently in the library of the University of Chicago and the Newberry Library.

If I could thank all those who encouraged me in my search to the point of the present book it would take several pages. But I cannot fail to mention gratefully the name of my teacher and friend, Andrew Papagiannopoulos-Palaios who gave me the first instruction and valid arguments on the problems of Athenian topography and epigraphy and who walked with me over every part of the old city important to them. Also I am deeply indebted to my late teacher, a noble scholar, Anton Ch. Chatzis who guided my first steps toward the study of Greek inscriptions. The present form of the book and its final printer's manuscript would never have been possible without the arguments and most valuable editorial assistance offered me by Miss Alyce Cresap who spent much time and effort on the manuscript of this book. Many thanks are due to her.

Finally I also owe thanks to John Damianos and John Daskalakis of the Greek Art Printing Company, who agreed to help me to prove to American scholars that scholarly Greek texts can indeed be typeset in the United States of America.

I hope that the reader will now be able to know and realize at once what I have learned after searching through sources for a number of years. In a study of such a character as this, the most important element is the basic group of testimonia and topographical identifications which, if they are correct, will be supported and made even stronger by the testimonia from texts and inscriptions which will be discovered and published in the years to come. Especially in the case of the details of the Agora in the old town, many new things are expected to be found in future excavations which will teach the truth and clarify those problems which have not yet been finally taken care of by the evidence at hand. For the topographical details of the Agora in Kerameikos, there are still many problems to be solved, especially in excavations to the north, northwest and southeast sides where many answers await the excavator's spade.

AL. N. OIKONOMIDES

CHICAGO, ILLINOIS
SEPTEMBER, 1964

INTRODUCTION

Athens is one of the oldest areas of active archaeological interest. The study of its ancient topography, with the Acropolis as the center of interest, has grown outward in all directions in an attempt to gather all possible evidence leading to a better knowledge of the city and the life of its citizens. A thorough study of the city's topography can teach us much of what transpired there during the many centuries when Athens was the cultural capital of the ancient world.

One of the oldest and most significant problems in the study of the topography of ancient Athens is the history of the changes in the location of the civic and commercial center of the city known as the Agora or marketplace. In the early nineteenth century, when the only guides available to researchers were ancient literary references and a few epigraphical texts, the problem was conveniently solved by placing the Agora and its buildings somewhere "around the Acropolis." Later, in what might be called a second period of research, the first systematic archaeological excavations were begun and numerous inscriptions were found. This caused the problem to rise again and it is to this period that we owe our foundations for the scientific study of the topography of ancient Athens as well as the first interpretations and theories resulting from the combination of literary references with archaeological evidence. There was still not enough of the latter, however, to adequately counterbalance the overwhelming number of literary references. The third period of study began with the excavations of the American School of Classical Studies in Athens in the area of the Agora in Kerameikos between the Temple of Hephaistos (the so-called Theseion) and the Stoa of Attalos, north of the Acropolis. When completed these excavations will have revealed the most impor-

tant parts of the civic center and the northern section of
the ancient city, a great and important step in our search
for knowledge of Athenian topography. From the beginning
of the American excavations until recently the location of
the Agora was considered to be solved due to the identifiable
discoveries of ancient shrines, administration buildings and
great numbers of inscriptions and other antiquities. From
these excavations we can truly understand for the first time
some of the ancient texts. It has become possible, for instance,
to retrace, nearly step by step, much of the route of the
second century A.D. author Pausanias, who has provided us
with the greatest amount of literary information on Athenian
topography as well as on most other cities of Greece of his
time.

However, these excavations which finally solved the problem of the location of an Agora in Athens "in Kerameikos,"
which was visited and described by Pausanias, actually
created a new problem, for no public building nor shrine in
the excavated area has been found antedating the early fifth
century B.C. Yet we have no doubt that an Agora existed in
Athens prior to that time for it is an archaeologically proven
fact that Athens had a settled population even before 3000
B.C.; thus we must search anew, this time for the location of
an earlier Agora than that of Kerameikos which apparently
did not come into being until the fifth century B.C. Moreover,
it would appear that this area in Kerameikos was insignificant
in the public life of the earlier Athenians. Where then was
the center of public activity in the city which was protected
by Athena, goddess of wisdom, and by the bravery of the
descendants of Theseus? Where was the Agora which was the
center of events prior to the victories of the Persian wars
which led to Athens' achievement of the cultural and military
leadership of ancient Greece?

THE TRANSFER OF THE ATHENIAN AGORA
FROM THE AREA OF THE ENTRANCE
OF THE ACROPOLIS TO KERAMEIKOS

From a study of the chronology of the archaeological evidence found in the excavations of the American School, a fair knowledge of ancient history, and the necessary amount of logic, we can proceed in our search for the location of an earlier Agora. But first, it is interesting to examine the possible reasons for the removal of the Agora from an earlier site to Kerameikos.

According to the rules of city-planning, one of the most likely reasons for such a major move might have been a population explosion causing the city to outgrow its boundaries and necessitating the creation of new civic facilities for a larger number of people. However such a population explosion is not historically supported in Athens prior to the first quarter of the fifth century B.C. Although the city was experiencing steady growth prior to this time, and we must accept the fact that houses were built on the outskirts of the city toward the north, there is nothing to indicate that there was a special need for transferring the city's Agora just to serve this "suburban" population which had, after all, existed outside of the old city even as early as the seventh century B.C. It would seem that the growth of the city did not assume great enough proportions to warrant a change in the city plan until some time later.

Secondly, history has shown that ancient city planners and governments were necessarily conservative when considering major moves of this sort, for the area of their potential activities was limited to that which could be enclosed within the ring of a protective wall. Only a major disaster, natural or man-made by enemies, could convince the people and their magistrates of the need for so great a change. In the aftermath of such disasters their natural inclination would have been to rebuild in such a way as to avoid any recurrence of the misfortune. History does not supply us with any information on such a disaster in Athens before the sack of the Persians in 479 B.C.

The city plan of ancient Athens, until the second century A.D., can be divided roughly into five stages. It began as a simple settlement on the Acropolis, later enclosed by the Pelasgic wall. Next appeared the settlement of the slopes bounded by the construction of the Pelargikon ring wall. The third city was the "new city" built following the triumphal period of activity after the victories of the Persian Wars, nearly ten times larger than the previous city and protected by the Themistoclean wall. Then came the little known extensions and limitations of the city plan during the fourth and third centuries B.C., followed by the revival of the ancient glory of Athens under the supervision of the Antonine emperors. This was marked by the reconstruction of the Themistoclean wall and the extension of the city to the wall of Hadrian. The stage in this evolution during which an adjustment of the city limits became necessary and during which the Agora or civic center might have been moved logically to a location more appropriate to a larger city can be definitely located at the beginning of the third period. This conclusion is supported not only by logic and history, but, as must be expected, by archaeological finds, epigraphical and literary texts, and discoveries in excavations, as will be explained below.

During this period there was the element of a major disaster which could have provided the impetus for changing the city plan. The city was looted, maliciously destroyed and burned by Persian invaders in 479 B.C. When the victorious Athenians returned triumphantly to their homes, having defeated the barbarians of the Great King, they were confronted by the still smoking remains of what once had been Athens. Their romantic attachment to the historical and religious traditions of Athens, plus the ready supply of building materials to be found among the ruins, caused the people to rebuild on the same site along the lines of a completely new city plan of which we still know only part. The Acropolis hill surface was enlarged by means of the embankments marked by the Themistoclean and Cimonian walls, a new wall ring was built for Piraeus, boundary stones, nearly uniform in size, fixed the various points of the areas within the city to be built and the plans of Cimon and Themistocles for the embellishment and fortification of the "new Athens" were carried out. This would seem to have been the most opportune time to relocate the Agora, transferring it from its original site at the entrance to the Acropolis to the open space below the hill of Agoraios Kolonos in Kerameikos.

The boundary stones of the Agora, as well as those from Kerameikos, and many others found in Athens, are roughly dated in the "first half of the fifth century B.C." A good many of them can be dated more specifically between 479-475 B.C., the years during which the new city plan of Athens was approved by the boule and put into motion by the placement of these markers amidst the ruins of the old city as well as out in the new fields which were to be newly incorporated within the enlarged area surrounded by the new city wall.

We have too the element of the people's dissatisfaction with the fortifications of the Acropolis and the old city foundations. The Athenians were evidently justifiably disappointed with the Pelasgic walls of the Acropolis and the Pelargikon which had permitted the enemy to enter the city "at their ease." A quotation from the Delphic Oracle especially for the occasion, "Let the Pelargikon be out of use," may have been used to thwart a weak opposition to expansion during the city planning discussion in the Athenian boule. Today we may suspect that the god of Delphi spoke once again according to the wishes of Themistokles, even as it had several years before in the famous oracle of the "wooden walls."

This was also a period of expanding population. Many Athenians who had lived in the countryside demes prior to the Persian invasion undoubtedly considered the possibility of another invasion, and having to rebuild their homes in any case, decided to do so within the new city walls where there would be an organized defense, or at least an evacuation plan, in case of danger. This influx of country people into the city would surely have created a need for a larger city area. Bear in mind that the Persian Wars were not yet over when the new city was laid out, and the fleet of two hundred triremes had not yet been put "into mothballs." The men still enlisted in the fighting of the second phase of the war certainly would have felt better knowing their families to be living safely within the new walled city rather than defenseless out in the countryside demes.

THE AGORA AT THE ENTRANCE TO THE ACROPOLIS

Possibly dating from the period of the earliest settlement on the Acropolis hill, the "ancient Agora," (see TA I, XVIII), although overshadowed by the Agora in Kerameikos, was one of the important areas in the city of Athens up to the first century B.C. By the fifth century B.C. the term used to designate the area around the Acropolis which had been the city before the Persian destruction was still "polis" in the sense of meaning "the old town "(TA XVIII), and the old civic center was still important to the religious life of Athens, for in it were preserved the sacred places of the most ancient traditional Attic and Ionian cults and rites.

A better understanding of the existence and the meaning of "the Agora in the old town" and its role in the public life of the Athenians is of major importance in any study connected with the ancient city of Athens. For from this ancient Agora originated some of the local Attic cults which later became Panathenian and Panhellenic and from the religious feasts, assemblies and festivals held here the dithyramb and the drama were born.

Perhaps one of the most important contributions of the study of this old Agora is to the political history of the city. The "old Agora" was the center for all of the known political activities of the early Athenian politicians and demagogues; in this place circles of men discussed their revolt against tyranny and later the first ostracisms, as well as the building of the first Athenian fleet. The most ancient public administration buildings were here and political figures such as Solon, Kleisthenes and Peisistratos knew no other agora or civic center in the city of their times. In those days the area of the hill Kolonos was simply land belonging partially to the demes of Melite and Kerameikos which contained a few farmhouses, wells and open fields. It was a place where some of the residents, following an old custom, preferred to bury their dead rather than carrying them to Kerameikos, even as late as the late sixth century B.C.

Although the Persians destroyed the walls, buildings and shrines and burned the old city in 479 B.C., the history of the Agora at the entrance to the Acropolis does not end there. For a number of years, from the time of the return of the Athenians until the official transfer of the Agora to the area below the hill of Kolonos which then became "Agoraios" (of the Agora), we must assume that public life was still active in the old civic center. And even after the transfer, while the affairs of the market and government were carried on in the new location, the old Agora remained important in religious observances. New altars and shrines were erected to replace those destroyed by the Persians and the religious traditions and sacrifices continued in their traditional places. The ephebes still took their oaths in the sanctuary of Aglauros. The young brides still had to take the water for their bridal baths from the nine-spouted fountain house and later dedicated the vases, especially made for the occasion, to the shrine of the "Bride," the daughter of Erechtheus who became the connecting link between the Ionian and native elements by giving birth to Ion (TA XXIV).

When Cimon brought the alleged remains of Theseus from Skyros he first established a sacred place for them in the old Agora; then a hero-shrine in the new (TA 30). When the cult of Asklepios was brought from Epidaurus it was located in the august area of the paternal cults in the old Agora for the Athenians he was not a foreign or barbarian god. As a son of Apollo Pythios (the Apollo Patroos of Athens), the god of medicine was also a revered half-brother of Ion, the ancestral hero. However, Amphiaraos, the Argive hero and divine medical competitor of Asklepios, did not secure a place in the old civic center although his cult came to Athens about the same time. His was politely placed in the new Agora (TA 7) where it remained more for the sake of appearance than for actual worship at least until the time that its existence was recorded by Pausanias.

In short the Agora of the old town remained a revered and active religious center, until the first century B.C., although it was not *"the* Agora" anymore. Then, after the alliance of Athens with Mithradates and the bloody sack of the city by Sulla (87 B.C.) during the long siege of Aristion in the fort of the Acropolis, this area suffered the most severe destruction of its history. Most of its temples and shrines were destroyed. In the years following a few repairs are known to have been made, especially in the Asklepieion and the temple of Aphrodite Pandemos (cf. TA III), but the old glory had finally faded. So, in the second century A.D., when the wealthy Athenian Herodes proposed to build a roofed memorial theatre honoring his wife Regilla in the ruined area, no one is known to have voiced any strong object-ions. The erection of the new Odeion in the area of the "Agora in the old town" caused some cults to merge with others, some to be transferred to new locations, and others to be housed under the same roof with another, though still separately worshipped and maintained. Apparently the Athe-nians of this period cared more for a new theatre in the city than for the preservation of the traditions of the holy sites revered by their ancestors.

When Pausanias visited Athens in the second century A.D. it seems that the preparatory work for the foundations of the new Odeion of Herodes were under way. The traveller, ascending the Acropolis, visited the temple of Aphrodite Pandemos (cf. TA. III) and the merged shrines of Demeter Chloe and Ge Kourotrophos (TA. VII), but he said nothing of the other cults known to have existed in the same area

according to inscriptions and other remains found in excavations many centuries later. Still, we cannot say that he
simply neglected to record them, for few have ever been so
precise and complete in their observations and descriptions
as was Pausanias. It must have been that these cults were
no longer in their original places. Surely Pausanias, whose
authority is seldom if ever doubted, never would have
dreamed that one day archaeologists would doubt the veracity
of Thucydides and other earlier authors in their writings
concerning the area, simply because he himself had failed
to mention something. If he had suspected this turn of events,
he surely would have made mention of the previous existence
of these cults, even though he did not see them, in order to
assure later scholars of their existence. It would have been
unbelievable to him, as it is to me, that strong arguments
could exist against the very being of these places, archaeologically and epigraphically known, simply because he did not
record them.

EXCAVATIONS, TEXTS AND CONFUSION

The collection and the understanding of the available
topographical testimonia from the existent literary and epigraphical texts is the most important background material
for the interpretation of finds from excavations. Inasmuch
as the ancient city of Athens is one of the basic places for
the search of knowledge pertaining to ancient Greek civilization, history and religion, one might expect that all of
the necessary preparatory work would have been accomplished
long ago with new finds merely supplementing the basic information from time to time, thus keeping the archaeologist
well informed, free to excavate, and well able to give valid
interpretations to his discoveries.

Actually such a work exists only for the Athenian Acropolis proper. This is *Arx Athenarum,* compiled by the German
scholars A. Jahn and Adolf Michaelis, published in 1901 at
Bonn. Naturally the epigraphical sources have increased in
number since its publication, but the work is still valid and

has a very complete collection of the available information from all literary sources and inscriptions discovered up to the time of its publication. For the topography of ancient Athens in general, the only available collection of literary and epigraphical sources is the *Schriftquellen zur topographie von Athen* by A. Milchhoeffer, published in Berlin in 1891 as a supplement to *The History of the City of Athens* by Ernst Curtius.

The valuable information from the thousands of inscriptions discovered since 1891 has not yet been used systematically in the study of Athenian topography. The most recent effort to do so was in 1931 when the second edition of *Topographie von Athen* by W. Judeich was issued. This was recently reprinted, but without changes. Unfortunately the second World War deprived us of the benefit of an index to the "editio minor" of the Attic inscriptions published in the series of the *Inscriptiones Graecae* which would have been of enormous help in the topographical studies of scholars not well acquainted with the use of the epigraphical sources.

Thus an archaeologist's knowledge of the literary and epigraphical sources on Athenian topography is still largely based on the same information which was available to him at the end of the nineteenth century, plus whatever research he may have done himself. Concerning the topography of the early Agora "in the old town" and the later Agora in Kerameikos, the available collections have been of small help, for the scholars who compiled them knew almost nothing of the actual topography of the area below the hill of Agoraios Kolonos as it has been revealed in the excavations of the American School of Classical Studies. Furthermore, before the excavations little was known about the possible dates of the buildings of the Agora in Kerameikos, and the "old Agora" mentioned in the fragment of Apollodorus (which we have called "the Agora of the old town") could not be considered as an important clue to the evolution of the city plan of Athens. When the temple of Aphrodite Pandemos was incorrectly "placed" "somewhere to the northwest of the

Acropolis," considerable confusion arose. The two Agoras were thereafter considered as one and few suspected that information in the ancient sources concerning things "in the Agora" might have meant another Agora than the one known to have been in Kerameikos.

With this scanty heritage of background information of the general topography of Athens, the excavations of the American School have been carried on for nearly three decades. In all fairness to the scholars involved these were the first systematic and careful excavations to be undertaken in the city of Athens. The only errors which occurred were some few misinterpretations of the finds due to misunderstandings of the literary and epigraphical sources. But, as most archaeologists know, this is not uncommon in any effort to reveal the deeply buried past of a civilization.

In 1957 Volume III of the series *The Athenian Agora. Results of the Excavations Conducted by the American School of Classical Studies at Athens* was published containing *The Literary and Epigraphical Testimonia* as collected by R. E. Wycherley. This has been considered by scholars to be the most complete collection of its kind and has received most laudatory reviews in the classical journals. The volume contains translations of the collected Greek and Latin passages into English. While this is not common, it is very useful in this "Greekless age" as the late Dr. Walter Miller of the University of Missouri called the twentieth century in his *Daedalus and Thespis*, the first collection of testimonia to offer Greek passages translated into English.

However complete and valuable Wycherley's work, I have some objections to the system followed in the arrangement of the collected citations, but even more to the fact that he apparently chose to judge some of the sources as to their value and then omitted several which might well have been included. If the size of the volume prohibited the inclusion of all the necessary references, I believe that his judgment should have been different in some cases. In other instances it appears that the compiler forced the source evidence to agree with the topographical theories of the Agora staff. It is a common practice to look for evidence confirming one's beliefs, but one's mind must never be closed to alternate possibilities. Perhaps my greatest disappointment in the collection by Wycherley is the omission of much published material from the earlier excavations in the area between the north slope of the Acropolis and the area of the Agora in Kerameikos, as well as from the Agora itself. There are also many literary texts, papyri and good editions of such well-known authors as Hypereides, Plutarch, Demades and others which apparently eluded the author, for I cannot believe they were deliberately omitted. Finally, I submit that Wycherley has misunderstood the references pertaining to the ''Agora in the old town'' which led him to some misleading conclusions.

In an effort to place finally the two Athenian Agoras in their proper locations the present work is now being published after a delay of several years. It may be of help in a general revision of *Agora III* which is undoubtedly being considered in order to include the many additional inscriptions which have been published in *Hesperia* since 1957 when Wycherley's work was first published.

The present work has been divided into two sections. The first contains the testimonia concerning the ''Agora in the old town,'' and is, as far as I know, the first attempt to collect the information from literary and epigraphical sources and to interpret them through archaeological evidence as a contribution to the knowledge of the topography of this particular area. I regret that many of the inscriptions and much archaeological evidence which would have been valuable have not yet been published by the Greek Archaeological Service which carried out the most recent excavations on the south slope of the Acropolis, so that they could have been included here. The testimonia of this first section are identified by Roman numerals.

The second section contains a collection of testimonia referring to the Agora in Kerameikos which either were not collected or were misinterpreted in *Agora III*. In a few cases

epigraphical material from the Agora inscriptions published
after the compilation of testimonia by Wycherley has been
used where necessary to clarify certain topographical details
of the two Agoras. The testimonia of this second section are
numbered with Arabic numbers. At the beginning of each
unit a reference has been made where applicable to *Agora III*
as WT, followed by page and quotation numbers to indicate
where the other testimonia relative to the subject have been
published.

Translations in English have been provided in both sections
of the work. Internal references are indicated by the abbre-
viation TA followed by a Roman numeral for testimonia of
the first section or Arabic numbers for those of the second.

It is hoped that this small volume will be of help to
scholars who will make the study of Athenian topography
one of their research subjects in the future. The earth of
Attica still holds many secrets. There are many inscriptions
as yet unpublished and excavations will reveal more and more
in the years to come. If what little I have succeeded in col-
lecting in the following pages contributes to the realization
of the need for more organized excavations to the south of
the Acropolis in order to study the ''Agora of the old town''
and leads to a better understanding of the finds from recent
excavations of the Agora in Kerameikos, its mission will be
accomplished.

The area of the Old Town is indicated by heavy dots (Pelargikon) on the assumed plan of the city by J. Travlos for the period 600-479 B.C. Note that the Pelargikon ring wall indicated by a broken line in the earlier plan has been forced to include the later Agora in order to accomodate recent theories. Location of cults verified topographically by excavations are marked by +. Those not so marked indicate possible locations, supported by literary and epigraphical texts.

+1. Nike Tower
 2. Demeter Chloe, Kore-Ge Kourotrophos-Blaute
+3. Aphrodite Pandemos - Peitho
 4. Herakles? Apollo Pythios? Themis
+5. Enneakrounos fountain - Asklepieion
 6. Theseion (Temenos)
 7. Sanctuary of Aglauros
+8. Sanctuary of Nymphe (Creusa)
 9. Orchestra, bleachers
 #   Assumed open spaces for assemblies

+10. Dionysos
+11. Zeus Meilichios (Agoraios, Eleos, Philios)
 12. Anakeion?
 13. Gate of Pelargikon to Melite
 14. Prytaneion, Epalxeis, lawcourts
+15. Eleusinion
+16. Later Enneakrounos
+17. Houses and family cemetery until early 5th c. BC
 18. Altar of Erinyes
+19. Propylon

THE AGORA IN THE OLD TOWN

APHRODITE PANDEMOS AND THE
INTERRELATION OF THE CULTS IN THE AGORA
OF THE OLD TOWN

I. Harpokration   1st or 2nd c. A.D.

Πάνδημος Ἀφροδίτη. Ὑπερείδης ἐν τῷ κατὰ Πατροκλέ-
ους, εἰ γνήσιος. Ἀπολλόδωρος ἐν τῷ περὶ θεῶν πάνδημον φησιν
Ἀθήνησιν κληθῆναι τὴν ἀφιδρυθεῖσαν περὶ τὴν ἀρχαίαν ἀγορὰν διὰ τὸ ἐνταῦθα πάντα τὸ δῆμον συνάγεσθαι τὸ παλαιὸν ἐν
ταῖς ἐκκλησίαις, ἃς ἐκάλουν ἀγοράς.

*Pandemos Aphrodite (mentioned by) Hypereides in the
speech "against Patrokles," if correctly ascribed to him.
Apollodoros in his book "about the gods" says that the epithet 'Pandemos' (of all people) was given to the (cult of
the) goddess established in the area of the old agora because
there all the people (pas Demos) gathered of old for their
assemblies which were then called 'Agorae.'*

In WT. 731 (pp. 224-5) the value of the information given
in the fragment of Apollodoros quoted in Harpokration about
the " old agora" (Wycherley's appellation for what we term
the agora in the old town) is challenged. "A site near the
entrance to the Acropolis would be a natural and probable
one for a primitive agora; but its character and contents are
almost wholly hypothetical," comments Wycherley who apparently has not questioned the possibility of definite information on the subject being available from other sources. This

attitude is a necessary one in his special case, because he had already used testimonia referring to the old agora near the entrance of the Acropolis as building material for his unrealistic theories of the "Orchestra" (WT 524-528) and "the primitive theatre in the agora" (WT. 728, p. 221), taking away from the "old agora" and the south slope of the Acropolis everything, even the poplars (WT. 720-728, pp. 219-221) and the bleachers (WT. 524-525, 528, 721, 723, 726, 727).

The question which always arises among those who choose to ignore the evidence of the literary sources and try to remove the old agora at the entrance to the Acropolis is, "Why doesn't Pausanias mention this old agora?" The answer is a simple one, having the evidence from the most recent excavations in this area. Pausanias, as is evident from his mention of the Odeion of Herodes (VII 20, 6), was in Athens during the preparations for the construction of its foundations, so the one and only sanctuary there which he could visit in the area was that of Aphrodite Pandemos (see TA, III). He also mentions the common sanctuary and the priests for the cults of Demeter Chloe and Ge Kourotrophos (see TA VII).

The location of the sanctuary of Aphrodite Pandemos is no longer open to suggestion and imaginary topographical interpretation (see *Ergon* 1960, pp. 10-13; figs. 9-14). The excavations carried on below the Nike tower produced all of the inscribed, pictorial and sculptural archaeological testimonia necessary to locate the sanctuary at last in the very place where it was supposed to be according to literary and epigraphical sources.

There are many considerations which can lead us to the conclusion that the foundations of a building just above the Odeion (See my map of *Akropolis*, Athens 1958, No. 38) are possibly and probably related to a temple of Aphrodite Pandemos. 1) Finds related to the cult of Aphrodite Pandemos dated at the 4th c. B.C have been found which had slidden downhill, (cf. TA. V) together with an inscribed dedication of the same period to Zeus Agoraios (see TA. XXXIX). 2) Pausanias visited the sanctuary of Aphrodite Pandemos, and noted the absence of the old statues, thereby indicating the existence of a sanctuary in the same location before his visit (see TA. III). 3) The possible destruction of the sanctuary with its temple, dedications and statues during the first Mithradatic War (88-86 B.C.) together with the other shrines in the same area (See Ervin, M., ''The Sanctuary of Aglauros on the South Slope of the Akropolis and its Destruction in the First Mithradatic War'' in *Archeion Pontou* 22, 1958, pp. 129-166). This third point would explain why Pausanias did not have an opportunity to visit more shrines of the old agora, and also gives rise to the possibility of the construction of a new sanctuary of Aphrodite Pandemos after the 1st c. B.C. on the site of the old one.

II. *Ergon* 1960, p. 12, fig. 14   early 4th c. B.C.

[- - o]ν Ἀφροδίτη[ι Πανδήμωι]

(*woman's diminutive name- -o)n to Aphrodite (Pandemos)*)

The inscription restored above according to the formula for dedicatory inscriptions can also be restored differently by using the formula of the inscriptions of sacred possessions. If, instead of the nominative of a woman's diminutive name ending with N, we will restore HIERO]N (Sacred), and instead of the dative we restore the name of the goddess in the genitive AphrodITH[S, the restored epithet would also be in the genitive making the following text:

[Ἱερὸ]ν Ἀφροδίτη[ς Πανδήμου]

(*Sacred) of Aphrodite (Pandemos)*)

The dedication is carved on a piece of black-glazed plate which can be dated to the early 4th c. B.C. The form of the letters agrees with this dating as do the other published sherds from red figured pottery excavated at the same spot. We can recognize Aphrodite depicted on at least two of

them (*Ergon* 1960, p. 11, fig. 9) and on the larger fragment
is a woman dedicator approaching the standing goddess. A
flying Nike painted on another red figured sherd is possibly
an additional testimony to the topographical relationship of
the cults of Nike and Aphrodite Pandemos, as they are related pictorially by the vase painter. The wing and the hair-
dress of a Nike appear also behind the figure of Aphrodite
in the best red figured fragment of the lot.

According to the report of the excavation (*Ergon* 1960),
pp. 10-11, fig. 10) there are fragments of 4th c. B.C. lekythoi
shaped as Aphrodite and Eros, terra cotta statuettes of
Aphrodite and Eros, and pieces from painted decorative
architectural parts also dated in the 4th c. B.C., all finds of
the same lot and as yet unpublished. Shells carved in the
rock for dedications on this side of the Acropolis were
observed for the first time in the progress of this excavation.

III. Pausanias I. 22, 3   2nd c. A.D.

'Αφροδίτην δὲ τὴν Πάνδημον, ἐπεί τε 'Αθηναίους Θησεὺς
ἐς μίαν ἤγαγεν ἀπὸ τῶν δήμων πόλιν, αὐτήν τε σέβεσθαι καὶ
Πειθὼ κατέστησε. τὰ μὲν δὴ παλαιὰ ἀγάλματα οὐκ ἦν ἐπ' ἐμοῦ,
τὰ δὲ ἐπ' ἐμοῦ τεχνιτῶν ἦν οὐ τῶν ἀφανεστάτων.

῎Εστι δὲ καὶ Γῆς Κουροτρόφου καὶ Δήμητρος ἱερὸν Χλόης·
τὰ δὲ ἐς τὰς ἐπωνυμίας ἔστιν αὐτῶν διδαχθῆναι τοῖς ἱερεῦσιν
ἐλθόντα ἐς λόγους.

*Aphrodite Pandemos as well as Peitho (Persuasion) were
established as cults from the time of the settlement by
Theseus, who united into one city the Athenian demes
(villages, townships). The old statues were not existent in
my time, but those I saw were the works of no inferior
artists. There is also a sanctuary of Ge Kourotrophos and
Demeter Chloe. About those epithets of the goddesses you
may learn by conversing with the priests.*

It is interesting that Pausanias visited the temple of
Aphrodite Pandemos and recorded that the cult statues were

not the old ones. The archaeological evidence (see TA. I, II) does not yet go back further than the 5th c. B.C. The facts that Aphrodite and Peitho are mentioned together, that Pausanias speaks of the missing *old statues* (ie. cult-statues) and the *statues* which he saw lead us to believe that the two old cults were under the same roof when he visited Athens. For Ge Kourotrophos and Demeter Chloe he definitely mentions *one* sanctuary. There are also other important primitive cults which he does not mention which we know were connected with these two goddesses. This is either because they were not particularly outstanding, or perhaps because they did not exist at that time. From inscriptions (see TA. XLII) we know that Ge Kourothophos was connected with the old cult of Blaute, and Demeter Chloe with Kore. The strange thing about this epigraphical evidence is that no known inscriptions on these cults can be dated after the latter half of the 2nd c. A.D. This fact can be interpreted in only one way to my knowledge, that being that the construction of the Odeion of Herodes in such a crowded area forced many of the ancient cults, shrines and sanctuaries to move to new locations or to merge (see TA. LIV).

IV. Diodorus Siculus 4. 62   1st c. B.C.

Φαῖδρα διὰ τὸ κάλλος ἐρασθεῖσα αὐτοῦ τότε μὲν ἀπελθόντος εἰς Τροιζῆνα ἱδρύσατο ἱερὸν 'Αφροδίτης παρὰ τὴν ἀκρόπολιν, ὅθεν ἦν καθορᾶν τὴν Τροιζῆνα.

Phaedra fell in love with him (Hippolytus) under the spell of his beauty, and when he left for Troezen she founded a sanctuary to Aphrodite upon the slope of the Acropolis in a place where there was a view toward Troezen.

From all of the testimonia connecting Phaedra and Hippolytus with an early cult of Aphrodite at Athens, this is the one which has some topographical value. The recent conclusions drawn from the excavations below the Nike tower (see TA. I-III) are that the temple of Aphrodite Pandemos was also called Aphrodite on Hippolytus due to its proximity to the so-called "sepulchral monument of Hippolytus" or "Hippolyteion" seen by Pausanias and mentioned just before the passage concerning the temple of Aphrodite Pandemos (Paus. I. 22, 1).

For the other passages see: Jahn, A., *Arx Athenarum*. 3rd ed. Bonn 1901, p. 40, 4* and Miller, W., *Daedalus and Thespis*. Vol. I., N.Y. 1929, pp. 152-155. An important observation of the excavations verifying the passage of Diodorus is that the earlier finds from the sanctuary of Aphrodite Pandemos had slidden down to a lower level (see TA I-II). The "spot where there was a view toward Troezen" makes my suggestion for the identification of the temple of Pandemos as the foundations just above the Odeion of Herodes more probable, as there would certainly have been no view if the temple had been located at a lower site. It is not necessary I suppose to note further than the actual possibility of a view of Troezen from the south slope of the Acropolis would be nil, even in the days of a totally unobstructed horizon, though it did face in the correct direction, and had the distance been less great and some mountains lower than the surface of the sea Phaedra might have seen her lover.

V. IG. II², 4596   4th c. B.C.

Τόνδε σοι, ὦ μεγάλη σεμνὴ Πάνδημε 'Αφρ[οδίτη - - κοσ]-
μοῦμεν δώροις, εἰκόσιν ἡμετέραις. 'Αρχῖνος 'Αλυπήτ[ο]υ Σκαμ-
βωνίδης, Μενεκράτεια Δεξικράτους 'Ικαριέως θυγάτηρ ἱέρεια
τῆς ['Αφροδίτης τῆς Πανδήμου, - - Δ]εξικράτους 'Ικαριέως
θυγάτηρ, 'Αρχίνου δὲ μήτηρ.

This, for Thee O great and revered Aphrodite Pandemos, we adorn with our statues as gifts.

Archinos, son of Alypetos of Skambonidae; Menekrateia, daughter of Dexikrates of Ikaros, priestess of (Aphrodite Pandemos); (Name - -) daughter of Dexicrates of Ikaros and mother of Archinos.

The discovery of this dedicatory inscription, together with
a decree dated in the year of the archon Euthios (283 B.C.,
IG. II², 657), and an inscribed fragment from an archaic dedication (IG. I², 700 - Reference ed. in Raubitschek, A.E.,
Dedications from the Athenian Akropolis, Cambridge, Mass.
1949. No. 296, pp. 318-320) provided the starting point for
moving the sanctuary of Aphrodite Pandemos from its original and actual place on the south slope of the Acropolis to
an uncertain spot somewhere "west of the Propylaea" where
it existed in the minds of many until the excavations of 1960.

These three inscriptions were found at the western foot of
the Acropolis "between the bastion of the Temple of Victory
(Nike) and the southern bastion of Beule's gate to the Acropolis. On the same site was found a large number of statuettes
of Aphrodite..." (See D'Ooge, M.L., *The Acropolis of Athens*,
New York, 1909, p. 260). Now if we consider the most likely
spot to which objects from the suggested site (see TA. I, IV)
of the temple of Aphrodite Pandemos would slide down, we
arrive at this very place and a topographical problem of
long standing appears to be finally solved. What remains to be
added is a detail concerning the reasons for anything sliding
from the high points of the south slope downward in all
directions. A reader of the "Memoirs" of General Makriyian-
nis, describing the siege of the Acropolis by the Turks (July
1826-June 1827) during the war of Greek Independence will
not wonder at all. Mines were exploded by both sides, and
the general bombardments and artillery fire on this particular
slope provide more than adequate reasons for slides large and
small of heavy stones as well as tiny fragments.

VI. IG. II², 5149   2nd c. A.D.

['Ιεϱ]έ[ας 'Αϕϱ]ο[δίτ]ης Πανδήμου, Νύμϕης, - -

For the priestess of Aphrodite Pandemos, the Bride, and - -

Having established the location of the sanctuary of Aphrodite Pandemos on the south slope of the Acropolis by means

of literary evidence and finds from excavations, we would
not regularly expect more evidence to be available. However,
when it exists, there is no reason not to bring it forth and
to examine its worth for the history and the topography of
the area.

The above inscription on a seat of the theatre of Dionysus
reserved it for the priestess of three cults: Aphrodite Pandemos, the Bride, and a third which has not yet been restored
satisfactorily. Now the one sanctuary of those excavated in
the Agora of the old town which is able to be exactly located
by a boundary stone 'in situ' is that of the Bride (Nymphe).
The existing excavation reports say that it was destroyed in
the 1st century B.C. What happened then to the old cult
which had been housed in it? The answer comes from the
inscription of the theatre seat. Simply, it was moved into
the nearby sanctuary of Aphrodite Pandemos when it was
restored. By the 2nd century A.D. (if the restoration by
Kirchner is correct), *one priestess* was serving both Aphrodite
and the Bride together with the third as yet unknown deity.

VII. IG. II², 5131   2nd c. A.D.

['Ιερε]ίας Κου[ρ]οτρόφου Δήμ[ητρος], Πειθοῦς.

*For the priestess of Demeter Kourotrophos and Per-
suasion.*

From what few things Pausanias says about the sanctuary
of Aphrodite Pandemos (cf. TA. III) we know that the cult
and the statue of Peitho (Persuasion) were housed in it at
the time of his visit. Also, he mentioned *one* sanctuary for
Ge Kourotrophos and Demeter Chloe.

This inscription mentions one priestess for *Demeter* Kourotrophos (evidently the same as *Ge* Kourotrophos) and Peitho. From this we may assume that the old cults of the area
had been crowded together into a small space and that there
were no longer individual priests and priestesses for each

one. So, although the cult of Peitho was in the sanctuary of
Aphrodite Pandemos, the priestess of Aphrodite already
served three cults. Therefore the duties of the priestess for
Demeter Kourotrophos must have been taken over by the one
who also served the cult of Peitho.

VIII. IG. II², 5152   2nd c. A.D.

Κουροτρόφου ἐξ 'Αγλαύρου, Δήμητρος.

(*For the priest of*) *Kourotrophos and of Demeter from*
(*the sanctuary of*) *Aglauros.*

A priest from the sanctuary of Aglauros was now serving
Kourotrophos and Demeter. This third theatre seat inscription
is good evidence that the Aglaureion was another of the sanctuaries destroyed and from which the priest and the cult had
to move and be combined with the cults in one of the remaining sanctuaries of Pandemos or Kourotrophos.

IX. IG. II², 5129   2nd c. A.D.

Δήμ[η]τρος Χλόη[ς ἱερέ]ως Διοφάντου.

For the priest of Demeter Chloe and Diophant.

A priest for Demeter Chloe appears in this inscription
having the additional title of *Diophantes*. To my knowledge
this title is known only epigraphically and can be explained
by means of the parallel, the well known title *hierophant* ἱερο-
φάντης (the one who teaches the rites of sacrifice and worship). Thus Διοφάντης Diophant would be either the one "who
teaches the rites of Zeus," or the one who performs a purification by means of the *dion* (cf TA. XXXV-XXXVII).

Having Zeus thus connected with the definitely chthonic
cult of Demeter Chloe, we may expect that the cult of Zeus
will also be chthonic. This is enough to locate for us the
literary source which explains the connection of the relation
of these two ancient deities with their locations in the Agora
of the old town. (cf. TA. X-XIII).

X. Pausanias I. 37, 4   2nd c. A.D.

Διαβᾶσι δὲ τὸν Κηφισὸν βωμός ἐστιν ἀρχαῖος Μειλιχίου Δι-
ός· ἐπὶ τούτῳ Θησεὺς ὑπὸ τῶν ἀπογόνων τῶν Φυτάλου καθαρ-
σίων ἔτυχεν λῃστὰς καὶ ἄλλους ἀποκτείνας καὶ Σίνιν τὰ πρὸς
Πιτθέως συγγενῆ.

*Across the Cephisus is an ancient altar of Zeus Meilichius
(Gracious). At this altar Theseus obtained purificaton at
the hands of the descendants of Phytalus after killing
brigands, including Sinis who was related to him through
Pittheus.*

XI. Plutarch, *Theseus*, 12. 1   ca. 46-120 A.D.

Προϊόντι δὲ αὐτῷ καὶ γενομένῳ κατὰ τὸν Κηφισόν, ἄνδρες
ἐκ τοῦ Φυταλιδῶν γένους ἀπαντήσαντες ἠσπάσαντο πρῶτοι, καὶ
δεομένου καθαρθῆναι, τοῖς νενομισμένοις, ἁγνίσαντες καὶ μει-
λίχια θύσαντες εἱστίασαν οἴκοι, μηδενὸς πρότερον αὐτῷ φιλαν-
θρώπου καθ᾽ ὁδὸν ἐντυχόντος.

*As he went forward on his journey and came to the river
Cephisus, he was met by men of the clan of the Phytalidae.
who greeted him first, and when he asked to be purifiied
from bloodshed, cleansed him with the customary rites,
made propitiatory sacrifices (Meilichia), and feasted him
at their house. This was the first kindness which he met
with on his journey.*

XII. Plutarch, *Theseus*, 23, 3   ca. 46-120 A.D.

Ἐξῃρέθη δὲ καὶ τέμενος αὐτῷ, καὶ τοὺς ἀπὸ τῶν παρασχόν-
των τὸν δασμὸν οἴκων ἔταξεν εἰς θυσίαν αὐτῷ τελεῖν ἀποφο-
ράς· καὶ τῆς θυσίας ἐπεμελοῦντο Φυταλίδαι, Θησέως ἀποδόν-
τος αὐτοῖς ἀμοιβὴν τῆς φιλοξενίας.

*Furthermore, a sacred precinct was also set apart (for
Theseus), and. he ordered the members of the families which
had furnished the tribute (to the Minotaur) to make contributions towards a sacrifice to himself. This sacrifice was*

superintended by the Phytalidae, and Theseus thus repaid
them for their hospitality.

XIII. Pausanias I. 37, 2   2nd c. A.D.

Μαρτυρεῖ δέ μοι τῷ λόγῳ τὸ ἐπίγραμμα τὸ ἐπὶ τῷ Φυτάλου
τάφῳ·
  ἐνθάδ' ἄναξ ἥρως Φύταλός ποτε δέξατο σεμνὴν
  Δήμητραν, ὅτε πρῶτον ὀπώρας καρπὸν ἔφηνεν,
  ἣν ἱερὰν συκῆν θνητῶν γένος ἐξονομάζει·
  ἐξ οὗ δὴ τιμὰς Φυτάλου γένος ἔσχεν ἀγήρως.

This story borne out by the inscription on the grave of
Phytalus:
"Hero and king, Phytalus here welcome gave to Demeter,
August goddess, when first she created fruit of the harvest;
Sacred fig is the name which mortal men have assigned it.
Whence Phytalus and his clan got honours immortal."

The four passages quoted and translated above will explain,
I believe, the connection of the cult of Demeter Chloe with
that of a chthonic Zeus and also with the temenos of Theseus
in the Agora of the old town.

The descendants of Phytalos are the earliest known clan
of Attica to be related with the cult of Demeter and the
meaning of their hero-ancestor's name is good proof that they
were connected with cult, related to planting and vegetation.

From the records of Pausanias and Plutarch we see that
they were connected too with the cult of Zeus Meilichios (the
Attic chthonic Zeus) and the earliest establishment of the
hero-cult of Theseus. So it is quite logical to recognize this
clan's right to bear a priestly title similar to the hierophant.
We must remember that the Phytalidae purified Theseus on
the altar of Zeus Meilichios. So when Theseus came into
power it is understandable that this friendly clan became
powerful too and that they would have installed their cults
of Demeter Chloe and Zeus Meilichios in the earliest Agora
of the city when it was settled anew by Theseus.

Now we can understand also why the Eleusinion was kept
far from the Agora in the old town. The early Athenian Demeter had already been firmly established in the religious life
when the union of Eleusis and Athens occurred requiring the
establishment of a 'mission' of the Eleusinian goddesses in
the city of Athens. It appears that the descendants of Phytalos did not recognize the right of a rival cult to be established in the Agora of the old town. Considering the fact
that they had in their hands the cults of Demeter, Zeus and
Theseus, they undoubtedly carried much weight in such matters and possibly even regulated them.

Now, especially since the discovery of two inscribed dedications to the early chthonic Zeus Meilichios of Attica in the
area of the Agora of the old town in excavations (TA XL),
it would seem that we have located the main site of his cult.
If so it is not difficult to see how this early cult of Zeus,
established in the Agora of the town, came to be called later
Zeus Agoraios.

XIV. Pausanias I. 22, 1   2nd c. A.D.

Μετὰ δὲ τὸ ἱερὸν τοῦ Ἀσκληπιοῦ ταύτῃ πρὸς τὴν ἀκρόπολιν
ἰοῦσι Θέμιδος ναός ἐστι. κέχωσται δὲ πρὸ αὐτοῦ μνῆμα Ἱπ-
πολύτῳ·

*After the sanctuary of Asklepius, as you go this way
towards the Acropolis, there is a temple of Themis. Before
it is raised a sepulchral mound to Hippolytus.*

I believe it is necessary to examine the temple of Themis
because the alleged tomb of Hippolytus was beside or in front
of it. This detail is important because from the recent excavations on the south slope (*Ergon* 1960, pp. 12-13) the
excavators came to the conclusion that the "Aphrodite on
Hippolytus" and "Aphrodite Pandemos" were one and the
same. The mention of a "temple" by Pausanias makes the
addition of topographical details impossible until the final
publication of the excavation reports.

It is possible to examine the interrelation of this cult with the others of the Agora in the old town from additional inscriptions on the seats of the theatre of Dionysus (cf. TA. XV-XVI).

XV. IG. II², 5130   2nd c. A.D.

'Ιερίας Γῆς, Θέμιδος.

For the priestess of Ge (Earth) Themis.

XVI. IG. II², 5098.   2nd c. A.D.

'Ερσηφόροις Β' Χλόης, Θέμιδος.

For the two Hersephoroi of Chloe (Sprout) and Themis.

XVII. IG. II², 5103   2nd c. A.D.

'Οληφόρου 'Αθηνᾶς, Θέμιδος.

For the bearer of the sacred basket of Athena Themis.

The information from these three inscriptions fits with the assumed relationship of Themis with the other known cults. The priestess of Ge (Kourotrophos) is seen to have had as an additional duty the care of the cult of Themis (TA. XV). Two "Hersephoroi" are connected with the cults of Chloe (Demeter) and Themis (TA. XVI) as is the bearer of the sacred basket with Athena Themis (or Athena *and* Themis). To relate these sacred personages to what we know of Attic mythology and the topography of the cults in the Agora in the old town is not difficult.

Near to the sanctuary of Aphrodite Pandemos was the sanctuary of Ge Kourotrophos and Demeter Chloe which Pausanias visited along his way and recorded (cf. TA. III). Perhaps Pausanias was eager to get on to the main sanctuaries of the Acropolis and did not pause to listen to the priests or perhaps he did stay to hear but lost his notes when he came to write his book on Attica (this has happened to modern scholars, certainly). In any case, all he wrote was, "You may learn about those epithets of the goddesses by conversing with the priests."

Not having the priests available today, the inscriptions on their theatre seats must suffice, and here is what we can learn from them.

The cult of Ge Kourotrophos is known as being related to the earth-born king-ancestor; we know the myth of the daughters of Cecrops (Herse, Pandrosos and Aglauros) being entrusted with a sacred basket containing the half snake baby Erichthonios by Athena. The only thing we don't know is the connection of Themis (Justice) with this myth, unless we accept her as the justification of the punishment of the two daughters (Herse and Pandrosos) of Cecrops who abused the divine law and opened the sacred basket. In any case, as the inscriptions indicate, there is some definite connection.

We also know that in the Agora of the old town there was a special sanctuary for the cult of Aglauros which later had to seek refuge in another sanctuary (cf. TA. VIII). In this special case, the priest of Aglauros became the priest of Kourotrophos and Demeter.

So it is indeed logical to have "Hersephoroi," "sacred basket bearer" and a priestess of Ge Kourotrophos and Themis all in the same place, and it is also expected that those early Attic cults were well connected with the Agora in the old town and the settlement by Theseus.

THE AGORA IN THE OLD TOWN,
THE FIRST ENNEAKROUNOS,
THE PELARGIKON

XVIII. Thucydides II. 15, 3-6   5th c. B.C.

Τὸ δὲ πρὸ τοῦ ἡ ἀκρόπολις ἡ νῦν οὖσα πόλις ἦν, καὶ τὸ ὑπ' αὐτὴν πρὸς νότον μάλιστα τετραμμένον. τεκμήριον δέ· τὰ γὰρ ἱερὰ ἐν αὐτῇ τῇ ἀκροπόλει καὶ ἄλλων θεῶν ἐστι, καὶ τὰ ἔξω πρὸς τοῦτο τὸ μέρος τῆς πόλεως μᾶλλον ἵδρυται, τό τε τοῦ

Διὸς τοῦ Ὀλυμπίου καὶ τὸ Πύθιον καὶ τὸ τῆς Γῆς καὶ τὸ τοῦ ἐν Λίμναις Διονύσου, ᾧ τὰ ἀρχαιότερα Διονύσια τῇ δωδεκάτῃ ποιεῖται ἐν μηνὶ Ἀνθεστηριῶνι, ὥσπερ καὶ οἱ ἀπ᾿ Ἀθηναίων Ἴωνες ἔτι καὶ νῦν νομίζουσιν. ἵδρυται δὲ καὶ ἄλλα ἱερὰ ταύτῃ ἀρχαῖα. καὶ τῇ κρήνῃ τῇ νῦν μὲν τῶν τυράννων οὕτως σκευασάντων Ἐννεακρούνῳ καλουμένῃ, τὸ δὲ πάλαι φανερῶν τῶν πηγῶν οὐσῶν Καλλιρρόῃ ὠνομασμένῃ ἐκεῖνοί τε ἐγγὺς οὔσῃ τὰ πλείστου ἄξια ἐχρῶντο, καὶ νῦν ἔτι ἀπὸ τοῦ ἀρχαίου πρό τε γαμικῶν καὶ ἐς ἄλλα τῶν ἱερῶν νομίζεται τῷ ὕδατι χρῆσθαι. καλεῖται δὲ διὰ τὴν παλαιὰν ταύτῃ κατοίκησιν καὶ ἡ ἀκρόπολις μέχρι τοῦδε ἔτι ὑπ᾿ Ἀθηναίων πόλις.

Before this (Theseus synoecism) what is now the Acropolis was the city, together with the region at the foot of the Acropolis toward the south. And the proof of this is as follows: On the Acropolis itself are the sanctuaries of the other gods as well as of Athena, and the sanctuaries which are outside the Acropolis are situated more in that quarter of the city, namely those of Olympian Zeus, of Pythian Apollo, of Earth, and of Dionysus in Limnae, in whose honor are celebrated the more ancient Dionysia on the twelfth of the month Anthesterion, just as the Ionian descendants of the Athenians also are wont even now to celebrate it. In that quarter are also situated still other ancient sanctuaries. And the fountain now called Enneakrunos, from the fashion given it by the tyrants, but which anciently, when the springs were uncovered, was named Callirrhoe, was used by people of those days, because it was close by, for the most important ceremonials; and even now, in accordance with the ancient practice, it is still customary to use its waters in the rites preliminary to marriages and other sacred ceremonies. And, finally, the Acropolis, because the Athenians had there in early times a place of habitation, is still to this day called by them Polis or city.

For some time this passage of Thucydides has been a veritable Procroustean bed for archaeologists and philologists,

being shortened or stretched as necessary to accomodate their
ideas on Athenian topography. Surely Thucydides, an Athenian who lived in the city for most of his life, would never
have thought that twenty five centuries after his death the
descendants of the Hyperboreans would suppose that he had
been incorrect in his observations of his native city. In any
case, the passage fits the topographic reality exactly as do
all the other passages of his history concerning the topography of Athens (cf. TA. XXXI).

One very interesting point of Thucydides' testimony has
never been thought to be of archaeological importance, I
believe, although it is. Writing during the time of the new
civic center, which had become more important than the
Agora in the old town devoted to old cults, he mentioned that
the Athenians "of Ionian ancestry" still celebrated the festival of Dionysus in the sanctuary "in Limnae" on the twelfth
of Anthesterion. Further, he mentions that the water of the
Enneakrounos was still used for sacred ceremonies and rites
connected with marriage in accordance with the old traditions and practices. In general we may well say that the
entire passage is his note on the survival of the old ancestral
sanctuaries and traditional ceremonies connected with them
in the "Agora of the old town."

Recent excavations have supplied evidence supporting and
proving the scholastic truth of the historian's statements. The
strange thing is that this appears to be the first time that
the excavation results have been put to this use. The sanctuary of the 'Bride' (Nymphe) (cf. TA XXIII) was discovered
just in front of the Odeion of Herodes. In and around it were
deposited thousands of fragments of black and red figured
vases (*Ergon* 1955, p. 11) and among them several 'graffiti'
or dedicatory inscriptions including 'sacred possesion' ones
mentioning the 'Bride' (Nymphe). It is not strange at all
to have found that the reconstruction of these vases in the
Acropolis Museum laboratory from the fragments resulted in
the most rare types of Attic vases called 'nuptial lebes' and
'nuptial loutrophoros,' both solely connected with Attic

marriage rites. Having definite proof produced by the archaeological spade as to the location of the marriage rites and
cults *exactly where Thucydides placed them,* we are forced
to accept also that the "Enneakrounos" fountain mentioned
by him as being connected with the bridal baths and ceremonies was in the same area. Thus, it is worthwhile to reexamine what the passage says about this fountain which
has been placed in every conceivable spot except its rightful
one in the last seven decades.

A "close by" fountain, the water of which was used "for
the most important ceremonials," can be no other than the
'fountain house' on the south slope by the Asklepieion. Its
architectural date agrees with the mention of "the tyrants"
(Peisistratidae) and the existence of special boundary stones
for it indicates its importance in religious rites (cf. TA.
XXVII). And to allay any further doubts, it is the unique
fountain in the area once known as "the Agora of the old
town."

The "enneakrounos problem" first appeared because of
Pausanias who wrote (I. 14, 1) that a fountain so called
and "adorned by Peisistratos" was on his route between
the definitely identified sites of the Odeion in the Agora and
the Eleusinion. This leaves no doubt that the fountain near
the church of the Holy Apostles (*Agora Guide* 1962, pp. 97-
98) was the Enneakrounos seen by Pausanias, but it also
seems that the name "Nine-spouted" was as common in
ancient Athens for a fountain house as are the toponyms in
America beginning with "Spring" (Springfield, Spring Val-
ley, Springdale, etc.).

It seems that Peisistratos was the first Athenian politician
to think that the population to the north of the Pelargikon
wall was entitled to a fountain house, and that the fountain
in the old town needed renewal. If we consider the fact that
the archaic pipeline which brought the water to the "out of
town" fountain house started from the area of old town
Agora (*Ergon* 1957, p. 8), the transfer of the name of the
spring fountain house is not difficult to explain. Even today in

Athens the water is called "Marathon" (as coming from the lake at Marathon) or "Oulen" (after the company which built the waterworks).

XIX. IG. II², 5006 a and b ca. 2nd c. A.D.

a.

Φοῖβος 'Αθηναίοις Δελφοὺς ναίων τάδε [εἶπεν]
ἔστιν σοι παρ' ἄκρας πόλεως παρὰ [τὸν προπύλαιον]
οὗ Λαὸς σύμπας κλήιζει γλαυκώ[πιδα 'Αθήνην]
Δήμητρος χλοίης ἱερόν, κούρη[ς τε μακαίρας]
οὗ πρῶτον στάχυς εὔξη[ται — — — — — —]
ᾶς πρότεροι πατ[έρες — — — — — — —]
ἱδρυσα[— — — — — — — — — — — —]

b.

[— — — — —]ν
[— — — —] ἀπαρχὰς
[— — — —]ς ἁγνοῦ
[— — — — τ]έχναισιν
[— — — — —] ἀνιούσης
[— — — — ϑ]ρεπτὰ
[— — — — — — — — λώι]ον ἔσται.

a.

Phoebus Apollo, the dweller of Delphi, said to the Athenians thus

In the area of Acropolis (high town) nearby (the Propylon) where the entire population celebrates honoring the bright-eyed (Athena), you have a sanctuary of Demeter Chloe (Sprout) and of the (blessed) Kore, where for the first time an ear of corn - - which your forefathers - - established - -

b.

- - first offerings . . . the holy . . . with arts - - ascending - - fed - - it will be better. ..

This inscription from a stele records an oracle addressed to the Athenians by the Apollo of Delphi, the "ancestral Apollo" of the Ionian segment of the population. We have here a poetic mention of a festival of Athena (not necessarily the Panathenaia) celebrated by "the entire population" in a spot near which was the sanctuary of *Demeter Chloe and Kore*. This inscription verifies that the cult of Kore (Sprout) is connected with the first ear of corn and thus reinforces the connection of the area with the group of early cults connected with Theseus and the priest-clan of the Phytalidae (cf. TA. X-XIII). The fragment gives only hints of the extreme importance which the completed text might give us as to the interrelation of the early cults on the south slope and the Agora of the old town.

We cannot say when the original oracle was delivered, but we know definitely now that its date was earlier than the first century B.C. when the sanctuary of Demeter Chloe and Kore was destroyed and fell to the level of a minor cult housed together with Kourotrophos at the time of Pausanias' visit (cf. TA. LI-LIII).

The theme and the vocabulary indicate that this oracle is one more case of an important document (5th c. B.C.?) being transcribed in Posteukleidian orthography and inscribed at a later date.

XX. IG. Il², 4762 a and b   1st-2nd c. A.D.

a.

Ὄσσε πάλ[ιν κλίνας — — —
Ἡρακλέους α[— — — —
αι δεκάδες πισ[τ — — — — —
ὑλιβάταισι Ἀ[γραυλίσι; — —
καὶ τοῦ ὁ[μοχόρου Πανὸς — —
Ἑρμε[ῖ προπυλαίῳ — — — —
AN[— — — — — — — —

b.

— — ἐκλ]ἐϊσεν ὁ Πύθ[ιος — — — — —
— — —]ων εὐσεβίης ἐτ[ιμᾶτο — — —
— — — —]υοῖς Ζηνὸς Γ[αιηόχοιο — —
— —]ων φλογὶ πε[ριθεὶς — —
vacat

a.

Having turned back his eyes - - of Herakles - - decades
of faithful - - to the forest walking (daughters of
Aglauros - - ?) and of (Pan who dances together - -?)
to Hermes (Propylaios - -?)

b.

- - the Pythian Apollo.
(made famous - -) he was honored with piety - -
- - to the sons of Zeus (the protector of the country - - ?)
- - putting the flame round - -

Another inscription of a poetic document can be connected
with the ancient cults on the slopes of the Acropolis. I have
restored the text based on this connection, but would like to
emphasize that even without a restoration we have here
mentions of Apollo Pythios, Herakles, Hermes, the sons of
Zeus, and someone or something burned by flames possibly
from a thunderbolt.

The two pieces of the inscription were found near the
theatre of Dionysus and are now in the Epigraphical Museum.

XXI. Callimachus.   3rd c. B.C.

Τυρσ<η>νῶν τείχισμα Πελασγικὸν εἶχέ με γαῖα

The earth held me, the wall of the Tyrrhenians, the
Pelargikon.

XXIa. Schol. Callimachus (*Pap. Univ. Milano* I, 93)

Ἱστορεῖ περὶ τῶν Ἀθήνησιν Πελασγικῶν ὅρων καὶ τοῦ
ποιηθέντος ὑπ' αὐτῶν τείχους.

He narrates about the Pelasgic area in Athens and of
the wall built by its boundary markers.

In the fragment of Callimachus the Pelargikon is connected once more with the confused Attic mythological tradition
about the "Pelasgians" or "Tyrrhenians" as digested and
understood by the Alexandrian poet. A question arises in

the interpretation of this fragment and that is if the last word
should be capitalized or not.

If capitalized the "Earth" (goddess) owned the Pelargikon
wall built by the Tyrrhenians which is quite different from
the wall being held by the earth.

Whichever it is, we have one more mention of the Pelargikon as Pelasgikon. And even more important is the note of
the scholiast saying that the wall was built from the boundary
markers of the Pelasgic area or "of the separate estates of
the Pelasgians at Athens and of the wall built by them."
In either case we must assume that the Pelargikon, still unknown archaeologically, was much later than the Pelasgikon
wall built on the Acropolis hill.

The problem of the Pelargikon wall is still unsolved as
far as archaeological evidence is concerned. Recently, from
excavations and research, we have gotten some possible hints
which may guide further searches. One of the most important
facts is that now the archaeologist's spade has reached the
area where the northern half of the Pelargikon ring wall
must have been and it should not be long before the excavation will have completely uncovered the areas east and
southeast of the Eleusinion.

For one more source supporting the existence of the Pelargikon cf. TA. XXI. It will not be surprising if the sanctuary
called "Leokorion" (cf. WT. 317-338, pp. 108-113) honoring
the daughters of the Attic hero Leos sacrificed for the sake
of the city, is somehow connected with this most ancient
defense wall as was the Prytaneion and one of the homicide
courts called Epalxeis (cf. TA 45).

XXII. IG. I², 76, 54-59 (GHI, I, 74)   445-416 B.C.

Τὸν δὲ βασιλέα hορίσαι τὰ ἱερὰ τὰ ἐν το|ῖ Πελαργικοῖ καὶ
τὸ λοιπὸν μὴ ἐνhιδρύεσθαι βομο[ὺ]ς ἐν τοι Πελα|ργικοῖ ἄνευ
τῆς Βο[υ]λῆς καὶ το[ῦ] Δέμο[υ] μεδὲ το[ὺ]ς λίθο[υ]ς τέ-
μνειν ἐκ τοῖ Π|ελαργικοῖ μεδὲ γὲν ἐχσάγεν μεδὲ λίθο[υ]ς. Ἐὰν
δέ τις παραβαίνει | τούτον τι ἀποτινέτο πεντακοσίας δραχμὰς
εἰσαγγελέτο δὲ h|[ο] βασιλεὺς εἰς τὲν βο[υ]λέν.

*And, the archon-king must delineate the boundaries of
the sanctuaries in the area of the Pelargikon and, from this
time on it is not allowed for altars to be erected in the
area of the Pelargikon without permission of the Boule and
the Assembly of the people, neither the destruction of the
stone blocks of the Pelargikon, nor to carry off earth or
to remove stones. And if someone disobeys one of the above
mentioned clauses he will have to pay a fine of 500 drachmas
and the archon-king must bring against him an impeach-
ment suit in the Boule.*

This passage is from the famous decree of Lampon and
speaks for itself. In the legal arrangements on problems connected with the first offerings to the Eleusinian goddesses and
other details connected with sacred things the Pelargikon
area is included. The only problem is the date of the document
(See Tod, GHI, I. pp. 184-185) which has unfortunately not
yet been fixed with certainty beyond the thirty years given.

THE AGORA IN THE OLD TOWN.

CULTS AND COMMODITIES

THE SANCTUARY OF THE "BRIDE" (NYMPHE)

XXIII. BCH 1958, p. 367, No. 5   Late 5th c. B.C.

Hόρος | Ηιερὸ | Νύμφης

*Horos (boundary marker) of the sanctuary of the
Bride (Nymphe).*

This inscription is one of the most important epigraphical
monuments for the topography of the "Agora in the old
town." It was discovered *"in situ,"* by the foundations of
the building for the cult of the Bride. The building is identified also by means of the thousands of black and red figured
vase fragments belonging to the type of "nuptial lebes"
(bridal basins) and "nuptial loutrophoros"' (bridal bath-
water jars) discovered in the excavations in and around the

sanctuary, some bearing inscriptions mentioning the "Nymphe." (cf. TA XVIII, XXIII-XXVI).

The inscription gives us our first opportunity to verify the testimony of Thucydides and the first hint toward the solution of the problem of the Enneakrounos. (cf. TA. XVIII, XXVII-XXVIII). The discussions of the problem of the identification of the Nymphe have already covered a respectable number of pages in newspapers, scholarly reviews and archaeological reports. One of the first was that of the employee of the Greek Archaeological Service who supervised the excavations and proclaimed that it was "an Attic cult unknown from literary and epigraphical traditions," and proposed that the sanctuary might belong to the nymph Oreithia.

Secondly in the first important and scholarly paper written on the subject (Ervin, M., "The Sanctuary of Aglauros on the South Slope of the Acropolis and its Destruction in the First Mithradatic War" in *Archeion Pontou* 22, 1958, pp. 126-166) it was proposed that the sanctuary belonged to the nymph Aglauros. This paper, well founded on the study of the literary, archaeological and epigraphical sources, has successfully established that the cult of. Aglauros was located in the area of the "Agora in the old town" and has proved that the cult of Oreitheia had nothing to do with the "Nymph" and her sanctuary (*loc. cit.*, pp. 130-131). But the author has wrongly concluded that the cult could be identified with the mythological tradition about the daughters of Cecrops and the sacrifice of Aglauros.

XXIV. Euripides, *Melanippe the Wise*, lines 7-11   5th c. B.C.

ἓν μὲν τόδ' ἐξέβλαστεν Ἕλληνος γένος.
πτόρθον δ' ἀφῆκεν ἄλλον εἰς ἄλλην πόλιν
[*Lacuna of one line..*]
κλεινὰς Ἀθήνας Ξοῦθον, ὧι Νύμφη ποτὲ
θυγάτηρ Ἐρεχθέως Κεκροπίας ἐπ' αὐχένι
Ἴων' ἔτικτεν.

One was the race which had sprung from Hellen's seed,
But he sent forth other shoots to other cities
[one lost line refers to Doros, the hero of the Dorians]
And Xuthus to the famous Athens, for whom the Bride,
the daughter of Erechtheus, bore Ion
on the slopes of Cecrops' citadel.

I do not think that this passage requires a long commentary, now that we know of the existence of a problem concerning the Nymphe (Bride) whose sanctuary was on the south slope of the Acropolis in the "Agora of the old town." The valuable testimony of Thucydides (TA. XVIII) indicates that the rites of Attic marriage of his time were definitely connected with this area according to the Ionian tradition. The finds of the excavations have verified it and now we need only the mythological background of the custom which is seemingly well established by the above quotation.

Logically the students of Attic cults have been puzzling until now over the reasons for the Athenian adoration of the Apollo of Delphi (Pythios) as "ancestral" because he was the father of Ion, the mythical ancestor of the noble Ionians, but no word was mentioned anywhere about a cult of his mother Creusa, the daughter of Erechtheus.

The tragedy "Ion" of Euripides has been studied as a piece of literature, but has never before been considered seriously as a document of Attic religion. Yet it is this play which gives the explanation of why the family tree of Ion had to be adjusted in the fifth century B.C. replacing his father Xouthos by Apollon, thus establishing the unity of the Ionian and Autochthon elements of the Athenian population and denying any common origins with Doros, the brother of Xouthos and the ancestral hero of the Dorians, hated by the Athenians.

It must be borne in mind that the Athenian audience of Euripides would have needed no mention of the name Creusa to know who "the Bride," the daughter of Erechtheus who bore Ion, was. The same was true of the officials who placed the boundary stones between the early Athenian shrines of the Agora in the old town. Everyone in the city knew then who the "Bride" was and they made no provisions to ease the work of later students of the area.

The misunderstanding of the actual meaning of this passage from the prologue of *Melanippe* is reflected in the introduction by A. S. Owen to the edition of "Ion" (Oxford. rp. 1957, p. xii) "in *Melanippe Sapiens* an unnamed daughter of Erectheus weds Xuthus and becomes mother of Ion."

The survival of the old tradition concerning the father of Ion in the prologue of *Melanippe* can now be used as an indication that the play is definitely earlier than the beginning of the Peloponnesian war (431 b.c.) and that "Ion" can be accurately but roughly dated between 431 and 406 b.c. The proposed date for the latter of 418 or 417 seems possibly correct although arrived at on the basis of literary and metrical criteria (cf. A. S. Owen, *loc cit.*, p. xli).

XXV. Schol Aristophanes, *Birds*, 1527

Πατρῷον τιμῶσιν 'Απόλλωνα 'Αθηναῖοι ἐπεὶ "Ιων ὁ πολέμαρχος 'Αθηναίων ἐξ 'Απόλλωνος καὶ Κρεούσης τῆς Ξούθου [γυναικὸς] ἐγένετο.

The Athenians have a cult of Apollo Patroos (Ancestral) because Ion, their polemarch, was born to Apollo and Creusa (the wife) of Xuthos..

The scholium which is not included in the testimonia for the cult of Apollo Patroos (WT. pp. 50-53, T. 107-113; TA.8) is interesting as a direct literary reference to the union of Creusa and Ion with Apollo Patroos. It is also important because the editors of Aristotle's *Constitution of Athens* (cf. H. Oppermann, Leipzig-Teubner 1928, p. 99, Fr. 1) have considered it as an echo of Aristotle's text about Ion in the lost section of his work, and as connected with the text of Harpokration on Apollo Patroos (WT. 110).

Wycherley, in his commentary (WT. p. 51) does not mention the *Ath. Pol.* as its source although the text of

Harpokration says that it is based on Aristotle. Thus, in his testimonia on the cult of Apollo Patroos (WT. 107-113) are not included any of the four texts which are later variations of the Aristotelian tradition: Bekker, *Anecdota Graeca*. 292, 3. - Schol. Plat. *Euthydemus*. 302c. - Lex. Patm. p, 143 (Sakkelion).

XXVI. Euripides, *Ion*, lines 276-280   ca. 418/417

ΙΩΝ πατὴρ Ἐρεχθεὺς σὰς ἔθυσε συγγόνους;
ΚΡΕΟΥΣΑ ἔτλη πρὸ γαίας σφάγια παρθένους κτανεῖν.
ΙΩΝ σὺ δ' ἐξεσώθης πῶς κατασιγνήτων μόνη;
ΚΡΕΟΥΣΑ βρέφος νεογνὸν μητρὸς ἦν ἐν ἀγκάλαις.

ION: Thy sisters did thy sire Erechtheus slay?
CREUSA: He endured to sacrifice them for his land.
ION: How wast thou only of thy sisters saved?
CREUSA: A babe new-born in mother's arms was I.

This quotation is interesting for it gives a hint as to the interpretation of two Attic dedicatory reliefs, one of which was found in the Acropolis excavations. Having established the existence of a cult of Creusa as the "Bride" earlier than the 5th century B.C. worshipped by the Athenians in the Agora of the old town, we might well expect to find records in Attic art of the myth about Creusa and her sisters.

On a relief dated ca. 540 B.C. which was found on the Acropolis (Acropolis Museum. 720. See Casson, Catalogue of the Acropolis Museum, vol. II; Ervin, *Aglauros*, pp. 151-152; Carpenter, R., in *AJA* 54, 1950, p. 324) is pictured a group consisting of a man leading three girls, the last of whom holds the hand of a small nude figure. This is a simple picture of a child and cannot be identified as either a boy or a girl. It would seem that this scene fits the myth about the daughters of Erechtheus as recorded by Euripides and Apollodorus (III. 15, I). Erechtheus leads his *four* daughters, Procris, Chthonia, Oritheia and Creusa as "babe new born" as she might have been represented by a primitive sculptor.

The unique parallel, as far as I know, is a relief in the Naples Museum (Ervin, *loc. cit.*) dated at the late 3rd century B.C. On it are shown six girls dancing in a line and holding the hand of the last girl *is a little girl.* Every possible interpretation has been given this relief except this one which actually fits. Here we have an artistic record of the later form of the myth of the daughters of Erechtheus. It is a work of art by an artist definitely inspired and impressed by the Euripidean tragedy *Erechtheus,* now lost to us, in which the daughters of Erechtheus were turned into stars by Athena (Euripides, Fr. 357). This is the constellation known as the *Hyades* with six primary stars.

The little child, definitely and unmistakably *a girl,* is Creusa following her sisters, increased in number, *Protogeneia, Pandora, Procris, Chthonia, Oritheia* and *Merope.* (For the relief see Horn, ''Stehende Weibliche Gewandstatuen in der Hellenistische Plastik,'' in *Rom. Mitt,* Erganzungscheft II, 1931, pl. 7).

ENNEAKROUNOS FOUNTAIN

XXVII. IG. I², 874   5th c. B.C.

Hόρος | κρένες

XXXIII. IG. I², 875   5th c. B.C.

[Hόρ]ος | [κ]ρένες.

Horos (Boundary markers) of the Fountain...

Having discussed previously the answer to the ''problem'' of the Enneakrounos (Nine-spouted) fountain in our commentary to the relative passage of Thucydides (TA. XVIII) as well as its connection with the Ionian tradition of marriage rites and ceremonies represented by the cult of the 'Bride' Creusa in the Agora of the old town (TA. XXIII-XXVI), little remains to be added concerning these two inscribed boundary makers (TA. XXVII is *''in situ''*.)

Epigraphically we may add that the dating of the two inscriptions, by means of the form of the letters, is thought to be not much earlier than the inscription of the boundary marker for the sanctuary of the 'Bride' (TA. XXIII) in which the appearance of the Η (*eta*) is not to my judgment a chronological indication of a date later than the year 403 B.C. On the contrary, it indicates that the "Ionic letters" were used in Athens earlier than the decree of Archinos which officially accepted them for use in state documents.

The fountain, was located definitely in the area of the Pelargikon, according to the clause in the decree proposed by Lampon (TA. XXII) *"to delineate the boundaries of the sanctuaries in the Pelargikon."* Even without considering the testimony of Thucydides and its relation to the Ionian rites and ceremonies and the excavation finds (TA. XVIII), there must have been a *sacred fountain,* if only to judge from the inscribed markers indicating its boundaries. And it is quite logical to assume that there was not another sacred fountain in the area in addition to the Enneakrounos or there would be some literary or epigraphical mention of it.

THE THESEION OR "TEMENOS"
(SACRED PRECINCT OF THESEUS)

XXIX. Aristotle, *Ath. Pol.*, 15, 4.   ca. 329-322 B.C.

παρεῖλε δὲ τοῦ δήμου τὰ ὅπλα τόνδε τὸν τρόπον. ἐξοπλα-
σίαν ἐν τῷ Θησείῳ ποιησάμενος ἐκκλησιάζεειν ἐπεχείρει, καὶ
[χρόνον προσηγό]ρευεν μικρόν, οὐ φασκόντων δὲ κατακούειν,
ἐκέλευσεν αὐτοὺς προσαναβῆναι πρὸς τὸ πρόπυλον τῆς ἀκρο-
πόλεως, ἵνα γεγωνῇ μᾶλλον. ἐν ᾧ δ' ἐκεῖνος διέτριβε δημη-
γορῶν, ἀνελόντες οἱ ἐπὶ τούτῳ τεταγμένοι τ[ὰ ὅπλ]α, καὶ
.[κατα]κλείσαντες εἰς τὰ πλησίον οἰκήματα τοῦ Θησείου, διε-
σήμηναν ἐλθόντες πρὸς τὸν Πεισίστρατον.

To take the arms away from the people he proceeded in the following way. He called for a muster of the citizens in arms at the Theseion, and there he began to address them; but after a short while, having given them the impression

*that his voice was not strong enough to reach them, he
asked them to climb up to the Propylon (gateway) to the
Acropolis where his voice could be better heard. While he
was gaining time by delivering his address, those he had
detailed to the task seized the arms and locked them in the
neighboring buildings of the Theseum, and then went to
inform Pesistratos with a sign.*

This text is very informative and interesting. Peisistratos
called for a muster of the citizens in arms at the Theseion.
The description certainly fits the location in the old town
"where the people gathered of old for their assemblies" (cf.
TA. I and XIX) *the old town Agora.* That the Theseion was
not the only sanctuary where assemblies were called by the
archons becomes obvious in the next testimonium by Polyaenos
in which there is, in the same story, confusion about the location. Instead of the Theseion we have there *Anakeion* as the
place for the "muster of citizen in arms" and instead of "the
neighboring buildings of the Theseion" we get the information that the seized arms were stored in the sanctuary of
Aglauros.

XXX. Polyaenos. I, 21, 2.   2nd c. A.D.

Πεισίστρατος Ἀθηναίων τὰ ὅπλα βουλόμενος παρελέσθαι
παρήγγειλεν ἥκειν ἅπαντας εἰς τὸ Ἀνακεῖον μετὰ τῶν ὅπλων,
οἳ μὲν ἧκον, ὃ δὲ προῆλθε βουλόμενος δημηγορῆσαι καὶ σμικρᾷ
τῇ φωνῇ λέγειν ἤρχετο, οἱ δὲ ἐξακούειν μὴ δυνάμενοι προελ-
θεῖν αὐτὸν ἠξίωσαν εἰς τὸ Προπύλαιον ἵνα πάντες ἐπακού-
σειαν, ἐπεὶ δὲ ὃ μὲν ἡσυχῇ διελέγετο, οἳ δ᾽ ἐντείναντες τὰς ἀκοὰς
προσεῖχον, οἱ ἐπίκουροι προελθόντες ἀράμενοι τὰ ὅπλα κατή-
νεγκαν εἰς τὸ ἱερὸν τῆς Ἀγλαύρου.

*(Peisistratos) wishing to take away the Athenians' arms,
sent word around that they should all come armed to the
Anakeion. This they did; Peisistratos came forward to
make a speech, and began to speak in a low voice. His
audience, not being able to hear him, asked him to go to
the Propylon, so that all might hear. Then, while he*

was talking quietly, and they were straining their ears to catch what he said, his bodyguard came forward, took up the arms and deposited them in the sanctuary of Aglauros.

The obligatory topographical conclusions from the comparison of the two texts are the following. Confusion appears as to the name of the sanctuary to which the citizens were called. This indicates that both the Anakeion and the Theseion were in the area of the *Agora in the old town*. Both traditions have preserved the Propylon of the Acropolis as the place to which the assembled citizens were transferred by the trick of Peisistratos, leaving their arms in the open space or square outside the Theseion or Anakeion. The buildings in which the tyrant's bodyguards hurriedly stored the arms are defined in the first sources as "the neighboring buildings of the Theseion," and in the second as "the sanctuary of Aglauros." This adds to the sanctuaries which existed in the Agora of the old town the Aglaureion, and explains the reasoning which guided Ervin (*Aglauros*, pp. 131-132) to assume that the sanctuary of the 'Bride' could be identified with the sanctuary of Aglauros. Actually, as far the location is concerned, all the sanctuaries mentioned can be included in what are called "the neighboring buildings of the Theseion" in *Ath. Pol.*

We may finally conclude that the Theseion in the Agora of the old town was a well known place. One more bit of information about it comes from Thucydides.

XXXI. Thucydides, VI, 61, 2   5th c. B.C.

καί τινα μίαν νύκτα καὶ κατέδαρθον ἐν Θησείῳ τῷ ἐν πόλει ἐν ὅπλοις.

And for one night they (the Athenians) even slept in in the Theseion of "old town" under arms.

The night mentioned is one of the month of terrorism and confusion after the famous case of the "Hermokopidae" (Mutilators of the herms) in the year 415 B.C. The passage

is a fine example of the confusion which can result when philologists lack knowledge of the archaeological topography and
fail to understand the author's topographical terms when
translating them.

The key to the passage is in the word *polis* (cf. TA. XVIII
& 29-30) which has the meaning here of "old town." Thus
it is not necessary to say that Thucydides "implies that
there were other shrines of Theseus *not* in the city" (WT.
359) nor to translate it as "in the precinct of Theseus within
the walls," (Tr. by Ch. F. Smith. Loeb. vol. III. p, 291) or
"in the Theseion in the city," (WT. p. 118).

It seems that the term *temenos* (sacred precinct) (cf. TA.
37) was the accepted one for the Theseion in the Agora of
the old town. I believe that in the topographic terminology
of the ancient Athenians the Theseion was the *temenos* of the
old town Agora, and such a term can be explained for the
place where the settler of the city was adored and where
his remains, allegedly found in Skyros, were buried. Thus
it is not strange that if the boundary markers placed to
delineate the area of the Theseion in the Agora of the old
town were marked simply as "boundary markers of the sacred
precinct" using the same logics the Enneakrounos would be
defined simply as "the fountain" (cf. TA. XXVII-XXVIII).

XXXII. IG. I², 860.   5th c. B.C.

    Ηόρος | το(ῦ) τεμένο(υ) [ς]

XXXIII. IG. I², 861.   5th c. B.C.

    Ηόρο[ς] | το(ῦ) τ[εμ]έ[νο(υ)ς]

XXXIV. IG. I², 862.   5th c. B.C.

    Ηόρος το(ῦ) τε|μένο(υ)ς

Of these three inscribed boundary markers as "*Horos of
the Sacred Precinct*," two were found in the area of the
Agora of the old town. The first, (TA. XXXII) is a find of
the excavations in the Odeion of Herodes, the second (TA.

XXXIII) of excavations on the south slope of the Acropolis, and the third (TA. XXXIV) was found in the old house of Finley by the church of St. Andrew.

The three boundary markers can be considered to be of the same date and of the same group of inscriptions as shown in the classification of Hiller in IG. I², even if only epigraphical criteria are used.

ZEUS AGORAIOS, MEILICHIOS, PHILIOS
(TA. IX-XIII, 42-45)

XXXV. Thucydides, I. 126, 4-7   5th c. B.C.

χρωμένῳ δὲ τῷ Κύλωνι ἐν Δελφοῖς ἀνεῖλεν ὁ θεὸς ἐν τοῦ Διὸς τῇ μεγίστῃ ἑορτῇ καταλαβεῖν τὴν Ἀθηναίων ἀκρόπολιν. ὁ δὲ παρά τε τοῦ Θεαγένους δύναμιν λαβὼν καὶ τοὺς φίλους ἀναπείσας, ἐπειδὴ ἐπῆλθεν Ὀλύμπια τὰ ἐν Πελοποννήσῳ, κατέλαβε τὴν ἀκρόπολιν ὡς ἐπὶ τυραννίδι, νομίσας ἑορτήν τε τοῦ Διὸς μεγίστην εἶναι καὶ ἑαυτῷ τι προσήκειν Ὀλύμπια νενικηκότι. εἰ δὲ ἐν τῇ Ἀττικῇ ἢ ἄλλοθί που ἡ μεγίστη ἑορτὴ εἴρητο, οὔτε ἐκεῖνος ἔτι κατενόησε τό τε μαντεῖον οὐκ ἐδήλου (ἔστι γὰρ καὶ Ἀθηναίοις Διάσια, ἃ καλεῖται, Διὸς ἑορτὴ Μειλιχίου μεγίστη, ἔξω τῆς πόλεως, ἐν ᾗ πανδημεὶ θύουσι, πολλοὶ οὐχ ἱερεῖα ἀλλὰ θύματα ἐπιχώρια), δοκῶν δὲ ὀρθῶς γιγνώσκειν ἐπεχείρησε τῷ ἔργῳ.

Now Cylon consulted the oracle at Delphi, and the god in answer told him to seize the Acropolis of Athens "at the greatest festival of Zeus." So he obtained a force from Theagenes and, persuading his friends to help, when the Olympic festival in the Peloponnesus came on he seized the Acropolis with a view to making himself tyrant; for he thought that the Olympic festival was not only the greatest festival of Zeus, but also in a manner was connected with him as having won an Olympic victory. But whether the oracle meant the greatest festival in Attica or somewhere else he did not go on to consider, and the oracle did not make it clear. For, in fact, the Athenians also have a festival in honour of Zeus Meilichios, the Diasia, as it is called, a very great festival celebrated outside the old town, whereat all the people offer sacrifices, many making offerings, sacrificing not the usual victims, but special ones of native breed. But Cylon, thinking that he was right in his opinion, made his attempt.

The fact that the festival of Zeus Meilichios in Athens was considered the greatest festival of Zeus verifies what has already been mentioned above about the cult which was considered to be worthy of a high priest with the title *diophant* (as parallel to the *hierophant*. cf. TA XXXVII) and was connected with the purification of Theseus, the hero settler of the city of Athens, from homicide (cf. TA. IX-XIII and TA. 33a-33e).

Zeus Meilichios is an autochthon deity symbolized by the bearded snake peculiar to Attic art and known from many dedicatory reliefs, inscriptions and other finds from Athens and Attica in general (cf. Harrison, J. E., *Prolegomena to the History of the Greek Religion.* 3rd ed. Cambridge 1922. pp. 13-28, 354, 358). From the inscriptions on the dedications we know surely that the chthonic Zeus symbolized by the bearded snake is also called *Ktesios Philios* and *Erkeios* and also that he is connected with the cults of Demeter and Kore.

XXXVI. Suidas.   10th c. A.D.

Διὸς κώδιον. θύουσί τε τῷ τε Μειλιχίῳ καὶ τῷ Κτησίῳ Διί, τὰ δὲ κώδια τούτων φυλάσσουσι καὶ Δία (δῖα) προσαγορεύονται, χρῶνται δ' αὐτοῖς οἵ τε Σκιροφορίων τὴν πομπὴν στέλλοντες καὶ ὁ δαδοῦχος ἐν Ἐλευσῖνι καὶ ἄλλοι τινὲς πρὸς καθαρμοὺς ὑποστορνύντες αὐτὰ τοῖς ποσὶ τῶν ἐναγῶν.

The "Kodion" of Zeus : They sacrifice to Zeus Meilichios and Zeus Ktesios, and they preserve the skins (of the sacrificial victims) which (are called) "Dia." And they are used both by those who prepare the procession of "Skirophoria" and the Dadouchos (torch bearer) in Eleusis and others (priests) for purifications by spreading them under the feet of those under a curse.

This passage connects the cult of Zeus Meilichios-Ktesios with the festival of Skirophoria. It is interesting to learn from other sources that in this old traditional Attic festival the priests of Erectheus (of the family of Eteobutadae) the priestess of Athena and the priests of Demeter and Kore were instrumental (cf. TA. XXXVII).

Thus the connection of the chthonic Zeus Meilichios with the oldest Athenian traditions and religious practices is beyond doubt. In a series of texts we are told about the cult's relation wth Demeter Chloe, Kore and Theseus (cf. TA. IX-XIII, XXV) and that his festival was a very great one in Athens. So we may expect the appearance of archaeological evidence which will visibly prove the existence of the cult in the Agora of the old town.

XXXVII. Eustathius, on *Odyssey*, xxii. 481   12th c. A.D.

Διοπομπεῖν δὲ ἑρμηνεύοντες φασὶν ὅτι δῖον ἐκάλουν κώδιον τυθέντος Διῒ μειλιχίῳ ἐν τοῖς καθαρμοῖς, φθίνοντος Μαιμακτηριῶνος μηνὸς ὅτε ἤγοντο τὰ πομπαῖα, καὶ καθαρμῶν ἐκβολαὶ εἰς τὰς τριόδους ἐγίνοντο. εἶχον δὲ μετὰ χεῖρας πομπόν· ὅπερ ἦν, φασί, κηρύκιον, σέβας Ἑρμοῦ. καὶ ἐκ τοῦ τοιούτου πομποῦ καὶ τοῦ ῥηθέντος δίου τὸ διοπομπεῖν...

Those who comment on the word 'diopompein' say the 'dion' was the appellation of the skin of a sacrificial victim offered to Zeus Meilichios during the purifications at the end of the month Maimakterion when they (celebrate the) procession called 'pompaia' and they are expelling at the 'trivia' (meeting of the three roads) the (so-called) purification offerings. And (the participants in this procession) carried in their hands the 'pompos' which was, according to what the commentators say, a 'caduceus' (herald's wand) for expression of respect for Hermes. And the verb 'diopompein' was produced from this 'pompos' and the 'dion' mentioned above.

This passage is of value because we know by means of the procession of 'purifications' and the mention of the 'purifi-

cation offerings' that the cult of Zeus Meilichios was also de-
fiinitely connected with *Hekate*, who, for several reasons, can
be considered as the *Kore* who was adored together with
Demeter Kore.

The 'diophant,' high priest of Demeter Chloe and Zeus
Meilichios, connects the ceremonial skin *dion* also with the
festival of *Skirophoria* (cf. TA. XXXVI) and the purifications performed by the 'Dadouchos' (torch bearer at
Eleusis).

XXXVIII. IG. II², 4786   2nd c. A.D.

[τύχηι]
ἀγαθῆι.

ὑψιμέδων ὕπατε, πάτερ Εἰρήνης βαθυκάρπ[ου],
σὸν Ἐλαίου βωμὸν ἱκετεύομεν ἡμεῖς
Θρήικες οἱ ναίοντες ἀγακλυτὸν ἄστυ τὸ [Σά]ρδω[ν],
Ἀρτεμίδωρος σὺν ἀδελφῷ τε κ[αὶ τεκέεσσιν?],
οὕνεκα οἱ ἐπένευσας ἰδεῖν [ἀ]λὸ[ς ἔκτοθι γαῖαν?].

O, Thou Dweller of the Heights, Supreme of gods,...
father of Eirene who gives increase to the crops, we
come to thy altar of Pity as suppliants, we Thracians who
live in the famous town of the Sardi, Artemidoros with his
brother and (children), because thou hast granted him to
escape peril on the sea and to reach the land.

This inscription is a dedicatory one on a relief which was
found in the excavations of the Odeion of Herodes. As even
Wycherley accepts, ''The halting verses appear to associate
Zeus with an altar of Eleos,'' (WT. p. 188). The idea of
''pity'' is easily associated with Zeus Meilichios, the epithet
of whom is sometimes translated into English as *Gracious.*
But we would like to underline the fact that the Zeus to
whom the relief is dedicated is the ''supreme one'' and is
also called the father of Peace who gives rich crops.

Logically we must associate this Zeus and his altar of Pity
with the cult of Zeus indicated by the *diophant,* the high
priest of Zeus and of Demeter Chloe (TA. IX) located in

36 THE TWO AGORAS

the area and connected by the priest clan of the Phytalidae
with the hero cult of Theseus as well (TA. XII).

XXXIX. *Bull. Corr. Hellenique* 82, 1958, p. 367   4th c. B.C.

'Ηδέα Διὶ Μιλιχίωι

Hedea to Zeus Meilichios.

The inscription is on a delicatory relief depicting the
bearded snake. It was found, as one might expect from what
is said in other literary and epigraphical sources, in the area
of the sanctuary of the 'Bride' (TA. XXIII-XXVI) and it
was lying on the bare rock level when found in the excavations
with the finds around and above it attesting to the fact that
this spot had been untouched and undisturbed in later periods.

The case of this relief is a good example of what may be
expected in an excavation when an employee of the archaeological service supervising it has no idea of the literary and
epigraphical source information (cf. *Ergon* 1957, p. 6: fig. 3
and p. 9). This inscribed find which helps in the understanding of the archaeological topography in the area, became a
minor 'list entry' of the records of the excavations rather than
receiving the attention it deserved as a possible guide to
more related articles of the cult of Zeus Meilichios.

As in the commentary on the inscription *BCH* (*loc. cit.*) we
can observe that the excavation supervisor was not the only
one who failed to realize the importance and meaning of Zeus
Meilichios and other ancient cults in the Agora of the old
town. This lack of knowledge is the major reason for our
scanty information concerning the archaeological finds and
topography of the oldest civic center in the city of Athens,
even though it has been excavated.

XL. *Ergon* 1960. p. 11, fig. 12   4th c. B.C.

Καλλίας Κα[- - Θο] -
ρίκιος, Θουκ[ριτίδης - - -]
Διὶ Φι[λίωι]

Kallias son of Ka - - of Thorikos (and)
Thoukritides - - - To Zeus Philios

The inscription was found in 1960 in the excavations in the area of the Agora of the old town "below the Nike Tower." To the same excavation period we owe the finds which solved the problem of the location of the sanctuary of Aphrodite Pandemos (cf. TA. I-VI) and new finds from the cult of the 'Bride.'

The identification of the cult of Zeus Meilichios and Zeus Philios is already an accepted fact which does not require additional comment (Harrison, J. E., *Themis.* pp. 297-313; *Prolegomena,* p. 359). The importance of the inscription lies in the fact that it is the third inscribed find from excavations verifying the existence of the cult of the chthonic Attic Zeus in the Agora of the old town where it was located according to indications in other epigraphical and literary sources. Zeus Meilichios, the greatest among the cults of the supreme god in Athens was *the* Zeus of the Agora in the old town. So it is no problem to see how he became Zeus *Agoraios* (cf. TA. 41-45) and the existence of an altar in the *Pnyx* and later in the Agora of Kerameikos and then in the two Agoras of Piraeus is a natural extension of his cult following the growth of the city of Athens.

How the "gracious" and "Friendly" chthonic Zeus later became the owner of the altars of Pity (TA. XXXVIII) will be no problem for the student of Attic religion. It is more problematic, I believe, to accept (as some of the excavators of the Agora blindly have) that the Altar of the Twelve Gods became the Altar of Pity after the 4th century B.C. when there is no written record, no literary or epigraphical source and no unbiased archaeological evidence existing to support such a theory (cf. TA 41).

It is really disheartening to find that the creators of this theory still insist upon it almost ten years after it has been rejected in a number of articles by valid and documented arguments based on archaeological evidence and literary and epigraphical sources. It is even more discouraging to read in the index of a book for the layman (*The Athenian Agora. A Guide.* 2nd ed. Athens 1962), "Pity (Eleos), *see* Twelve Gods," and to realize that the completely discredited theory still has its supporters publishing articles in 1964 which eliminate the opposing bibliography from their references. For this reason a note is needed on the alleged change of the Altar of the Twelve Gods of the Agora in Kerameikos to the Altar of Pity (Eleos) as mentioned by Pausanias.

The 'identifiication' was first proposed by Homer Thompson (*Hesperia* 21, 1952, pp. 47-82), who tried to connect with the alleged change of the Altar of the Twelve Gods to Altar of Pity, the originals (of which not a scrap has been found in the Agora, cf. *Hesperia* 33, 1964. p. 76) of the four known 'three-figure reliefs' (see Bibliography *Hesperia* 21, 1952, p. 60. note 35). This attribution has been convincingly discredited first by G. Zuntz (*Classica and Mediaevalia* 14, 1953, pp. 71-85) and later by N. Hausmann (*Griech. Weihreliefs*, 1960, pp.48-50) and W. Fuchs (*Die Vorbilder der neuattischen Reliefs*, 1959, p. 133).

The careful scrutiny of the information from literary and epigraphical sources on the Altar of the Twelve Gods by Stephen Koumanoudes (*Neon Athenaion* 1, 1955, pp. 159 ff.) has failed to show any gap in the continuation of the cult of the Twelve Gods in Athens from the 6th century B.C. to the 2nd century A.D. (although Thompson says we have no mention of it after the fourth century B.C.). The result of this study produced sources mentioning the altar dated later than the terminus for the alleged change (cf. *Athenaika* 16, 1960, p. 10, and TA. 41). Finally, the present writer concluded the re-examination of the sources (*Athene* 22, 1962, No. 4 pp. 42-43 and *Athenaika*, ibidem, pp. 1-13) with the result of realizing that the altars of Eleos in Athens were actually the altars of Zeus Meilichios, who was also known as Agoraios because of his cults in the Agora of the old town, in the Agora in Kerameikos and in the Agoras of Piraeus and other Attic demes.

XLI. IG. III, 285   2nd c. A.D.

Ἱερέως Διὸς Φιλίου

For the Priest of Zeus Philios

This inscription carved on one of the seats of the theatre of Dionysus can be considered as the closing point of the identification of the old chthonic Attic Zeus known as Agoraios, Meilichios, Ktesios, Philios with the cult of Eleos (pity). No inscription for a priest of the Attic Zeus under any of the other epithets (except Philios) appears on another seat, although it is well known that more than one priest or priestess served some of the old cults in the Agora of the old town in some cases. But what is even more important is that we do not have any mention of a special priest of Eleos (pity), either amidst the inscriptions of the seats or in any other inscription found in Attica.

KOUROTROPHOS AND BLAUTE

(TA. III, VII-IX, XVIII)

XLII. IG. II², 5183   1st c. B.C. (ante 86 B.C.)

Εἴσοδος πρὸς ση-
κὸν Βλαύτης καὶ
3 Κουροτρόφου ἀνει-
[μέ]νη τῷ Δήμῳ.

Entrance leading to the sacred precinct of Blaute and Kourotrophos devoted (let free) to the people.

This "guide" inscription was found below the Nike Tower, and this fact indicates that its evidence supports the location already given in the literary sources (TA. III, VII-IX, XVIII) for the sanctuary of Kourotrophos, which according to the more precise text of the inscription, was actually "a sacred precinct." But the appearance of Blaute, as a co-owner of this ancient site of a cult is a fact fully attested to by the inscription, but not recorded in any other source.

The dating of the earlier editors, to my knowledge, appears as late first to second century A.D. The form of the letters confirm that the document would be better placed in the early first century B.C.

XLIII. *Hesperia* 26, 1957, p. 91, No 40 1st c. A.D. (ante 86 B.C.)

[Εἴσ]οδος πρὸς
[σηκ]ὸν Βλαύ[της]
[καὶ Κουροτρόφου]
[ἀνειμένη — — —

(Translation same as that of TA. XLII)

This fragment of an inscription is exactly similar to the one in TA. XLII and was carved for the same purpose. It was found in the excavations of the later Agora in Kerameikos built into the wall of a modern house. This helps to illustrate better the well known fact that stones, both inscribed and not, were carried away from the south slope in later centuries for modern building purposes. The dating of this inscription must also be the first century B.C.

The main question arising from the two inscriptions (TA. XLII-XLIII) is concerning the deity called *Blaute*. What is available from both literary and epigraphical sources is no big help in the problem, we must admit. Although it would be convenient to accept, as others have, the proposed association of Blaute with Aphrodite (Ida T. Hill, *The Ancient City of Athens* p. 132, 237, note 24), a scholar's convenience is not valid in studying a problem.

XLIV. Hesychios   5th c. A.D.

Βλαύτη τόπος 'Αθήνησι.

Blaute a site in Athens.

XLV. Pollux, VII. 87   2nd c. A.D.

῟Ηρως 'Αθήνησιν ὁ ἐπὶ Βλαύτῃ

A hero in Athens, the one on Blaute (sandal?)

We gain only vague information from the two testimonia
(TA. XLIV-XLV). We learn from Hesychios that a site in
Athens was called Blaute, which might be a vague reference
to the sacred precinct of TA. XLII-XLIII, and in Pollux
we have a cult mentioned in connection with the site called
Blaute, or perhaps with the deity Blaute itself. From this
last reference and the connection of Blaute with a type of
sandal or slipper called *blaute* or *blaution* and a votive stele
found near the Asklepieion (Ath. N. M., No 2565) a large
amount of archaeological literature came into being, parts
of which can be justified now after what we have learned
about the snakelike representation of the chthonic Attic Zeus
Meilichios and his cult as "Agoraios" in the Agora of the
old town (cf. TA. IX-XIII, XXXV-XLI) and in the later
Agora in Kerameikos (TA 41-45).

From the known cults of the chain of relations between the
old Attic cults in the Agora of the old town, Zeus Meilichios
is closely connected with Demeter Chloe (TA. IX) and the
latter with Ge Kourotrophos (TA. III). Now Blaute, a deity
sharing the same sacred precinct with Kourotrophos, must
be logically connected with all of the other cults of the old
group of Attic deities.

As a consequence, the hero cult connected with Blaute possibly can be united with one or all of the known characteristics
of this special group of cults, i.e. purification from blood,
sprout and vegetation, and benefits from the earth. Continuing
in this direction for the location of the "Hero" we can get
some additional information from other unused sources.

Coming back to the relief on the votive stele found near
the Asklepieion (Svoronos, *Nat. Mus. of Athens*, Pl. LX), we
must reexamine its symbolism. The stele is nearly 8 feet tall.
A large sandal in relief is represented on the top part on
which is also sculpted the figure of a man dressed in himation.
On the lower part a snake is represented. Now, if the interpretation by Ch. Tsountas (*Arch. Eph.* 1906, pp. 243-248) is
reinforced by our identification of the snake as the symbol of
Zeus Meilichios-Agoraios, the symbol of the hero on the

Blaute (sandal) shows him in connection with Zeus Meilichios.
Considering the fact that the stele was found near the
Asklepieion and that the sacred precinct of Kourotrophos
and Blaute was nearby in the area of the Agora in the old
town, Tsountas' interpretation is made stronger and is
perhaps deserving of final acceptance.

From this point we can start again in our search for the
characteristic of the cult of the "Hero on Blaute," having
the assistance of the relief's identification for the connection
with Zeus Agoraios-Meilichios. The suspicion of a *purification*
hero connected with sprout and vegetation is now our lead
and the sources provide exactly the assistance we need.

XLVI. Plutarch. *Solon.* 12, 4   10th c. A.D.

Οὕτω δὴ μετάπεμπτος αὐτοῖς ἧκεν ἐκ Κρήτης Ἐπιμενίδης ὁ
Φαίστιος, ὅν ἕβδομον ἐν τοῖς σοφοῖς καταριθμοῦσιν ἔνιοι τῶν
οὐ προσιεμένων τὸν Περίανδρον. ἐδόκει δέ τις εἶναι θεοφιλὴς
καὶ σοφὸς περὶ τὰ θεῖα τὴν ἐνθουσιαστικὴν καὶ τελεστικὴν σο-
φίαν, διὸ καὶ παῖδα νύμφης ὄνομα Βάλτης καὶ Κούρητα νέον
αὐτὸν οἱ τότε ἄνθρωποι προσηγόρευον.

*Under these circumstances they summoned to their aid
from Crete Epimenides of Phaestus, who is reckoned as the
seventh Wise Man by some of those who refuse Periander
a place in the list. He was reputed to be a man beloved of
the gods, and endowed with a mystical and heaven-sent
wisdom in religious matters. Therefore the men of his time
said that he was the son of a nymph named Balte, and
called him a new Cures.*

XLVII. Suidas   10th c. A.D.

Ἐπιμενίδης... υἱὸς Βλάστας, Κρὴς ἀπὸ Κνωσσοῦ.

Epimenides... son of Blasta, a Cretan from Knossos.

The two testimonia (TA. XLVI-XLVII) refer to Epimenides, the most honored and well known purifier connected with
early Athenian history. He was the one who was called upon

to purify the city after the "Cylonian sacrilege" (ca. 636 B.C., cf. TA. XXXV) and who revised Athenian religious rites and sacrifices *"taking away the harsh and barbaric practices."* The name of his "nymph" mother has been definitely distroyed in both sources (*Balte, Blaste*) and the correction to *Blaute* is a perfectly apt restoration paleographically.

Pausanias (I. 14, 4, cf. WT. 198) saw a seated statue of Epimenides in front of the Eleusinion. If our identification of the renowned purifier with the "Hero on Blaute" is correct, this is one more testimony which Pausanias failed to mention because at the time of his visit (cf. TA. III, VII) the cult of Kourotrophos had already moved together with Demeter Chloe and nothing is known from that time on about Blaute or the "Hero on Blaute."

The Agora in the old town can be identified now as the scene of the "Cylonian sacrilege." We know from Aeschylus (*Eumenides*, lines 969-975) that between the altar of the Erinyes and the place of the cult of Peitho was the altar of Zeus Agoraios, and from Aristophanes (*Knights*, 1311-12, cf. WT. 341) that the Theseion or "temenos" in the old town was not far from the altar of the Erinyes. Thus, in the description of the slaughtering of the followers of Cylon (in Plutarch, *Solon.* 12) coming down from the Acropolis, it is said that they were attacked when the first of them reached the altar of the Erinyes. We can understand now more clearly what Plutarch meant when he said, *"Those who were outside were stoned to death, and those who took refuge at the altars were slaughtered there."* (IN the Agora in the old town).

Epimenides, the "beloved of the gods," the purifier of the Cylonian sacrilege, had much work to do in order to purify the shrines and altars of the old town Agora. So it is not strange that the Athenians decided to honor his "divine mother," the nymph Blaute, in the same area. (Bear in mind that he accepted no money for his holy work). Some centuries later it seems that Epimenides himself was honored in the same place. Now it also becomes significant that Blaute's cult was associated with Ge Kourotrophos (the Earth rearing the youth). As honors were due to Ge because she nursed Erechtheus, the hero king of Athens, so were similar honors due to the nymph Blaute who nursed and reared the heropurifier Epimenides, the "new Cures" of the Gracious Idaean Zeus.

DEMETER CHLOE AND KORE

XLVIII. Aristophanes, *Lysistrata*, line 835   411 B.C.

...παρὰ τὸ τῆς Χλόης

— — — *by the sanctuary of Chloe*

XLIX. Schol. Aristophanes, *Lysistrata*, line 835

Χλόης Δήμητρος ἱερὸν ἐν ἀκροπόλει, ἐν ᾧ οἱ Ἀθηναῖοι θύουσιν μηνὸς Θαργηλιῶνος, ὡς Φιλόχορος φησὶν ἐν ϛ.

A sanctuary of Demeter Chloe in Acropolis, in which the Athenians sacrifice in the month Thargelion, as Philochoros says in the sixth book ⸤of his Atthis⸥.

L. Schol. Sophocles, *Oedipus Coloneus*, 1600

Εὐχλόου Δήμητρος ἱερόν ἐστι πρὸς τῇ ἀκροπόλει. Καὶ Εὔπολις «Μαρικᾷ»: Ἀλλ' εὐθὺ πόλεως εἶμι θῦσαι γάρ με δεῖ Χλόῃ Δήμητρι.

A sanctuary of Demeter Euchloos is near the Acropolis. (Mentioned also) by Eupolis in (the comedy) "Marikas." But I am now going straight to the old town, because I must sacrifice to Demeter Chloe.

LI. Kornoutos, *Epidrome*, 28

Περὶ τὸ ἔαρ τῇ Χλόῃ Δήμητρι θύουσι μετὰ παιδιᾶς καὶ χαρᾶς ἰδόντες χλοάζοντα καὶ ἀφθονίας αὐτοῖς ἐλπίδα ὑποδεικνύντα.

During the beginning of the spring they sacrifice to Demeter Chloe with play and joy, having seen the sprouting (which) gives them a hope of abundance.

LII. IG. II², 4663   4th-3rd c. B.C.

[Δήμητρι Χλόηι κ]αὶ Κόρηι
[— — — —] *vacat* ἀνέθηκε
[ὁ τάδε ἐποίη]σεν.

To Demeter Chloe and Kore (name of donor) dedicated (Sculptor's name) made it.
On a fragment of a marble statue base now in the Acropolis museum.

LIII. IG. II², 4778   1st c. B.C.

       Δήμητρι Χλόῃ
       καὶ Κόρῃ
3   τὴν Κουροτρό-
       φον Εἰσίδοτος
       ἀνέθηκεν
6   κατ' ὄνειρον

To Demeter Chloe and Kore Isidotos dedicated this statue of Kourotrophos after a dream.

On a statue base found by the Beule's Gate of the Acropolis.

LIV. IG. II², 4748   1st c. B.C.

       Δήμητρι Χλ[όηι]
       καὶ Κόρ[ηι] Εἰ[σί]-
       δοτο[ς ἀνέ]θη[κε]
       χ[αριστήριον].

To Demeter Chloe and Kore Isidotos dedicated as a gift.

On statue base found on the Acropolis. Both TA. LII and LIII seem to be dedicated by the same individual. The earlier editors have dated them in the 2nd c. A.D., but our dating criteria can place them no later than the early first century B.C.

LV. IG. II², 4777   2nd c. A.D.

Δήμητρι Χλόῃ ἡ ἱέρεια [Νι]κοβούλη ἡ καὶ
'Ιλάρα Θεοτείμου ἐξ 'Ερμείου ἀνέθηκε.

*To Demeter Chloe, the priestess Nikoboule called also
Ilara (daughter?) of Theoteimos of Hermos.*

Found on the south slope by Keramopoulos in 1928. The
dating in the second century A.D. and the absence of Kore,
indicated that the dedication belongs to the period when the
cult merged with Kourotrophos (cf. TA. III, VII.)

HERAKLES

To my knowledge, no literary source mentions a cult of
Herakles in the area of the Agora in the old town, or in
connection with the ancient cults (for a possible exception
see TA. XX). It must be noticed that the same absence is
true of the later Agora in Kerameikos where the entire honor
to Herakles known to us is a single statue (cf. WT. 117)
which must also be considered as a relic of the cult of Hera-
kles-Dionysos, the thirteenth god voted for the sake of the
deification of Alexander the Great, and to which a statue
was erected (cf. TA. 34).

However, archaeological evidence from excavations would
indicate quite the opposite. Three inscribed dedications (TA.
LV-LVII) found on the south slope of the Acropolis, and
an inscription found in the excavations of the Agora in Kerameikos (possibly carried from the south slope, cf. TA XLIII)
are sound pieces of evidence which cover the gap in information from literary sources. If the inscription (TA. LVIII)
was not so definite a testimonium indicating the existence of
a sanctuary of Herakles, we could assume that the three other
dedications might have been related to what Plutarch wrote
on the interchange of the hero cults of Theseus and Herakles
(*Theseus.* 35, 2).

LVI. IG. II², 4611   end 4th c. B.C.

[Στράτων Στρ]ατοκλέους Λακιά-
[δης ἀνέθη]κεν Ἡρακλεῖ. Θεόδο-
[τος Στράτωνος], Κλεοφῶν Στράτωνος.

Straton, son of Stratokles of Lakiadae dedicated to Hera-
kles (and his sons with him?) Theodotos, son of Straton
and Kleophon, son of Straton.

Found on the ascent to the Propylaea of the Acropolis.

LVII. IG. II², 4571   344/3 B.C.

Θ ε [o ι]
[Μν]ησίστρατος [— — — — —]
['Αν]έθηκεν Ἡρα[κλεῖ — — —]
['Επὶ Λ]υκίσκο[υ ἄρχοντος — —]

The Gods. Mnesistratos — — dedicated to Herakles — —
in the year of (the eponymous) archon Lykiskos.

Found in the excavations of the south slope of the Acropolis.

LVIII. IG. II², 4613   end 4th c. B.C.

Λυσιστράτη
ὑπὲρ τῶν παίδ[ων]
Ἡρακλεῖ ἀνέθηκεν

Lysistrate, for the sake of her children dedicated to
Herakles.

Found in the excavations of the south slope of the Acropolis.

LIX. *Hesperia* 3, 1943, p. 64-65

[hι]ερὸν
[τὸ Ηε]ρακλέο[ς]

Sacred of Herakles

Found in the excavations of the later Agora in Kerameikos.

AGLAUROS AND THE NYMPHS
(cf. TA. VIII, XXX)

The study of testimonia from the sources related to the
cult of Aglauros definitely places this famous sanctuary where
the Athenian ephebes annually took their oaths in the Agora
of the old town. Ervin (*loc. cit.* p. 134-140) has already distinguished this cult and the name of Cecrop's daughter
Aglauros from the obscure cult on the north slope honoring
his wife *Agraulos*. This distinction will help in the restoration
of several passages in classical texts in which the copyists
understandably confused the two names *Aglauros* and *Agraulos* creating some real puzzles for the student of Attic mythology and topography.

The successful topographical interpretation of the passage
mentioning the cult of Aglauros in Herodotus VIII, 53 by
Ervin (*loc. cit.*, p. 133) and its connection with the topography indicated by Polyaenos (cf. TA. XXX) is a valid
contribution to the restoration of the south slope as the historical scenery for the sack of the Acropolis by the Persians
in 479 b.c. Also, the connection of the cult of Aglauros with
the cult of the Nymphs is another important discovery by
Ervin (*loc. cit.* pp. 142-159), who has also connected all of
the existent archaeological and epigraphical evidence resulting in an indication of the need for connecting those two early
Attic cults on the south slope of the Acropolis and the Agora
in the old town.

The three Cecropid nymphs are not to be confused with the
daughters of Erechtheus (cf. TA. XXVI) and the Hyakin-
thides or Geraistai Nymphai Genethliai, are also identified by
Ervin (in *Platon* 11, 1959, pp. 146-159) with the Nymph
sanctuary on the hill of the Nymphs and the fertility cult
which still survives under the auspices of ''Hagia Marina.''
It is interesting that the cult of the 'Bride' (cf. TA. XXIII,
XXIV·) can now be connected with the Erechtheid Nymphs
due to the testimony of Euripides (TA. XXIV) and not with
Aglauros and the Cecropid Nymphs as Ervin suggested.

EPILEGOMENA TO THE TESTIMONIA FOR
THE AGORA OF THE OLD TOWN

For a number of the cults and public buildings which possibly can be located in the area now established as the Agora in the old town, the first and oldest civic and religious center in the city of Athens, we believe that the few available testimonia are just a portion of what actually exists. The unfortunate habit of employees turned excavators to lock up and hide the sculptures, inscriptions and other finds for decades, often with no intention of publishing them, (e.g. the inscriptions discovered during the reinforcement and restoration of the Nike Tower, the inscriptions from Ilissos and the sanctuary of the Bride, etc.) creates a poor heritage for the generations to come and is not in keeping with my idea of duty to scholarship and research. Let us hope that it will not become "tradition" to keep what has been hidden in hiding nor to place new discoveries with them.

For the sake of fellow students of Athenian topography I have tried to keep up with what has been published, up to the moment that this book went to press. In some cases, for the sake of the necessary additions, certain secondary testimonia were replaced or omitted entirely, much to the dismay of printers, publishers and proofreaders, but the work had to end somewhere, and it is entirely possible, indeed likely, that additional testimonia could well be added.

The cult of Kourotrophos was also mentioned in the testimony of IG. II², 4757 (found by the Asklepieion), IG. II² 4869 (found by the entrance to the Acropolis) and IG. II², 4756 (found in the Asklepieion), none of which are included here. Also the reference to Aphrodite Pandemos from the dedication of Nausikrates (IG. II², 4862) found in a modern house on the north slope, used as a building block, and which was for a time considered as one of the places where adventurous topographers wished to place the sanctuary, has been omitted. The testimonia of the cults of Aglauros and the Nymphs were not repeated here (see Ervin, *Aglauros*). Finally, several of

the inscriptions from the seats of the theatre of Dionysus
have not been used in connection with either mentioned or
unmentioned cults associated with the Agora of the old town.
These and many more, I hope to include in my work in preparation: "Sources of History, Mythology and Topography
of Ancient Athens" to be published in the near future.

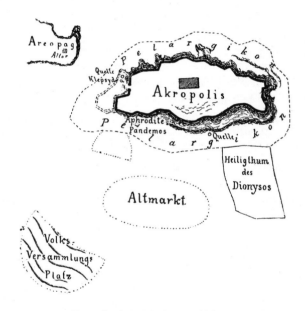

From Curtius, *Die Stadtgeschichte von Athen*

THE LATER AGORA
IN KERAMEIKOS

STOA ALPHITOPOLIS (Grain and Flour Merchants)

1. Aristophanes, *Ecclesiazusae*, Lines 684-686   391 B.C.

καὶ κηρύξει τοὺς ἐκ τοῦ βῆτ' ἐπὶ τὴν στοιὰν ἀκολουθεῖν
τὴν Βασίλειον δειπνήσοντας, τὸ δὲ θῆτ' ἐς τὴν παρὰ ταύτην
τοὺς δ' ἐκ τοῦ κάππ' ἐς τὴν στοιὰν χωρεῖν τὴν ἀλφιτόπωλιν

*And the herald will summon those under Beta to follow
to the Basileios Stoa to dine; those under Theta to the one
next thereto; and those under Kappa to pass to the flour-
merchants stoa.*

Three important stoas of the Agora are mentioned in this
passage. Two of these are known by name, the *Basileios Stoa*
and the *Alphitopolis Stoa*. The other stoa is simply mentioned
as being next to *Basileios*. For thoughts on the identification
of this "anonymous" stoa see WT. 7, note. The meaning is
clear enough that the three stoas are mentioned in their topographical succession.

Some scholars believe that the *Alphitopolis Stoa* was the
one known from other references as being near the docks at
Piraeus, but if this interpretation is to be accepted, we must
also accept the illogical fact that grain and flour were sold
only in Piraeus. Even if we want to agree, the parallel texts
to this passage will disagree with us. First of all, from the
inscriptions found in the Agora excavations, we find several
mentions of officials connected with the state control of the
grain trade. Secondly, there are definite references to the
grain and flour trades being carried on in the Agora, and

thirdly, it is absurd to suppose that grain and flour, the staples of the Athenian diet, were not sold where all other foods were sold, in the market of the city. The three lines above are used by Wycherley (WT. 7 and p 193), but without any comment on the location of the *Alphitopolis Stoa*.

2. IG. II², 836 Lines 1-4   a little after 229 B.C.

ΟΣ . . . ΔΙΚ[- - - - - σίτου]
τοῦ διαμε[τρουμένου - - - εἰς τὴν σ]
τοὰν τὴν ε[- - - τοῦ γυμνασίου τοῦ]
βασιλέως Π[τολεμαίου - - - - -]

Those who... measure the grain... in the Stoa which... (of the gymnasium of) king P(tolemy)...

The mention of a stoa is clear. This building was not far from Ptolemy's gymnasium, and probably was used occasionally for the counting of grain (cf. *Grain*). For other buildings used for the same purpose cf. Demosth., xxxiv, 39 (Pompeion) and xxxiv. 37 (Odeion of Pericles) and TA. 68-70.

MAKRA STOA

3. Schol. Aristophanes, *Birds*, 997.

Κολωνὸς ἐστὶν οὐ ἔτερος ὁ μίσθιος λεγόμενος. Οὕτως μέρος τι σύνηθες γέγονε τὸ Κολωνὸν καλεῖν τὸ ὄπισθεν τῆς Μακρᾶς στοᾶς, ἀλλ' οὐκ ἔστι. Μελίτη γὰρ ἅπαν ἐκεῖνο, ὡς ἐν τοῖς ὁρισμοῖς γέγραπται τῆς πόλεως.

It is not another(deme)Kolonos, the so-called "hired" one. For it is a common habit to call what is behind the Makra Stoa "Kolonos," but it is not. For all of this part is Melite as is depicted (on the plan?) on the boundaries of the city.

The scholiast was confused, for he knew that *"Kolonos"* was the name of an Attic deme, so he said that a work or plan "On the boundaries in the city" indicated the part where the *Makra Stoa* stood within the limits of the deme of Melite. But we know that according to IG. II², 968 (Line 14) the stoa was *in Kerameikos* which means "in the Agora area" (cf. Plutarch, *Sulla*, 14, 4—TA. 58, 59)

The error of the scholiast helps us to understand that behind the stoa was the hill of Agoraios Kolonos, and probably it was one of the stoas seen by Pausanias "*from the Two Gates* (Dipylon) *to Kerameikos*" (I. 2, 4; WT. 2).

ELEUTHERIOS ZEUS SHRINE AND STOA
(WT. pp. 25-31; T. 24-46)

4. Eustathius, *On Iliad*, I. 529   12th c. A.D.

Φέρεται ἱστορία, ὅτι Εὐφράνωρ ᾿Αθήνησι γράφων τοὺς δώδεκα θεοὺς καὶ ἀπορῶν πρὸς οἷον ἀρχέτυπον γράψει τὸν Δία, παρήιει ἐν διδασκάλου καὶ ἀκούσας τῶν ἐπῶν τούτων
᾿Αμβρόσιαι δ᾿ ἄρα χαῖται, καὶ τὰ ἑξῆς,
ἔφη ὅτι ἤδη ἔχει τὸ ἀρχέτυπον καὶ ἀπιὼν ἔγραψεν.

There is a story, according to which Euphranor, painting the Twelve Gods in Athens and being in a dilemma as to an original for painting Zeus, was one day in a teachers' (session) *and, having heard those verses*
Divine hair, etc.
said that he had the original and went straightaway and. painted the god.

For schools in the Agora area cf. *Biographi Graeci*, p. 265; Demosth., xviii, 129; Apollod. (WT. 340, 347, 456, p. 126).

5. Plutarch, *De gloria Athen*, 2   ca. 46 - ca. 120 A.D.

Εὐφράνωρ τὸν Θησέα τὸν ἑαυτοῦ τῷ Παρρασίου παρέβαλε λέγων, τὸν μὲν ἐκείνου ῥόδα βεβρωκέναι τὸν δὲ ἑαυτοῦ κρέα βόεια τῷ γὰρ ὄντι γλαφυρῶς ὁ Παρρασίου γέγραπται, καὶ πεποίηται καί τι προσέοικε τὸν δ᾿ Εὐφράνορος ἰδών τις εἶπεν οὐκ ἀφυῶς
Δῆμον ᾿Ερεχθῆος μεγαλήτορος, ὅν ποτ᾿ ᾿Αθήνη
θρέψε Διὸς θυγάτηρ

γέγραφε δὲ καὶ τὴν ἐν Μαντινείᾳ πρὸς Ἐπαμεινώνδαν ἱππο-
μαχίαν οὐκ ἀνενθουσιάστως Εὐφράνωρ.

*Euphranor used to compare his Theseus with the one
by Parrhassius saying that his competitor's Theseus appeared to have grown up eating roses while his own looked
as if Theseus had been eating beef steaks. And it is true
that Theseus is painted and conceived by Parrhassius in
an elegant way and looks like (what Euphranor said). As
for Euphranor's (painting), one of those who saw it quoted
pointedly:*

    The people of Erechtheus, noble in heart
    Fostered by Athene, the daughter of Zeus
*Euphranor has also painted, in an enthusiastic man-
ner, the cavalry battle (of the Athenians) with the forces
of Epameinondas at Mantineia.*

The antagonism of Euphranor against Parrhasius on the
paintings of the stoa is also clear from what is said by Pausanias (I. 3, 3; W.T. 30) about his personified Demos. We
know also from Pliny, xxxv, 69 that Parrhasius *"Pinxit De-
mon Atheniensium, argumento quoque ingenioso."* The painting of Euphranor's "Demos and Democratia" was probably
copied by the sculptor of the relief for the stele on which
the law addition proposed by Eukrates has been inscribed
(*Hesperia.* XXI, 1952, pp. 355-359). Another unpublished
relief of the same type exists in the Acropolis Museum
(possibly the work of the same sculptor).

6. Menander, *Phosphodees,* fr. 459 (Koerte)   342-290 B.C.

    Ἐπίσημον οὖν τὴν ἀσπίδα εἰς τὴν τοῦ Διὸς
    στοὰν ἀνέθηκαν

    *So they put an inscription on the shield and set it up in
the Stoa of Zeus.*

Koerte, in his commentary on the fragment, says "De armis
in porticu Jovis sacratis v. Pausanias X. 2p, 6," (WT. 32.
Also cf. Paus. I. 26, 2 — WT. 31).

POIKILE STOA
(WT. pp. 31-45; T. 47-98)

7. Clement of Alex., *Stromateis* IV. 19, 21   2nd-3rd c. A.D.

Μέμνημαι δὲ καὶ Κυνικῆς τινος, Ἱππαρχία δὲ ἐκαλεῖτο ἡ Μαρωνῖτις, ἡ Κράτητος γυνή, ἐφ' ἧι καὶ τὰ κυνογάμια ἐν τῆ Ποικίλῃ ἐτέλεσεν.

Among the women philosophers I recall a Cynic. Hipparchia was her name, from the city of Maroneia, the wife of Krates. On her he consummated the "Cynic's Wedding" (Kynogamia) in the Poikile Stoa.

Wycherley, in his commentary on Apuleius, *Florida*, 14 (WT. 52) says, "It is highly likely, in view of its position and associations, that the stoa is the Poikile." But the passage of Clement is clear; there is no doubt that the place was the Poikile.

AMPHIARAOS
(WT. p. 49; T. 105)

8. IG. II², 4441   a) lines 1-7 before 217/16 B.C.
    b) lines 8-12, 2nd c. A.D.

a. [Ἀμφι] αράωι καὶ Ὑγ[ι]είαι· | Τιμοκλῆς | [Σ]ωκράτου Ἁλαιεὺς | [ἱε]ρεὺς γενόμενο[ς] | ἐπὶ Εὐάνδρου | ἄρχοντος | ἀνέθηκεν.

b. Φίρμος (Φίρμου) | Γαργήττιος | Ἀσκληπιῶι | Ἀμφιαράωι | ἀνέθηκεν.

a. To Amphiaraos and Hygieia, Timokles, son of Sokrates of Halai, dedicated (this altar), ordained as priest the year of archon Euandros.

b. Firmus, son of Firmus of Gargettos, dedicated to Asklepios (and?) Amphiaraos.

A small marble altar found in the area of the Roman market bears these inscriptions. For the connection of Amphiaraos' cult with Hygieia cf. the introduction to the speech "In Defense of Euxenippos," in my edition of Hypereides ("Papyros," No 247, Athens 1958, pp. 43-48).

APOLLO PATROOS
(WT. pp. 50-53; T. 107-113)

9. Schol. Aeschines, I (*Timarchos*), 114

Τοὺς ὁρκίους] Ἀπόλλωνα πατρῷον καὶ Δήμητρα καὶ Δία, ὡς φησὶ Δείναρχος ὁ 'ῥήτωρ.

The oath-witnessing gods: Apollo Patroos, Demeter and Zeus, according to the orator Deinarchus.

Cf. Lysias, X. 17; Aeschines, I. 81, 88, 108; Demosth., IX. 65. 50, XIII. 21. 198; IG, I², 10, line 15.

For the cult of Creusa the 'Bride' see TA. XXIII-XXVI.

ARTEMIS PHOSPHOROS
(WT. pp. 56-57; T. 120-121)

10. IG. II², 4659   4th-3rd c. B.C.

[Ἀρτέμι]δι Φωσφόρ[ωι] | [—] κράτης | [- -] μέδοντος | ἀνέθηκεν.

To Artemis Phosphoros, - - krates, son of - - medon dedicated....

Inscription on a marble base found on the north slopes of the Acropolis. In opposition to Wycherley's statement that there are no literary references to Artemis Phosphoros in Athens itself (p. 57), at least one can be found quoted in Athenaeus III. 84, b, although it is not cited here since it is not of topographical importance.

PHOSPHOROI
(WT. pp. 57-59; T. 122-124)

11. IG. II², 4718   end of 2nd c. B.C.

<Ἐπ>ὶ <Ἄρ>χοντος Δ<ι->ονυσοδ[ώρ]ου . . . σι<ο>ς, θεαῖς <Φ>ωσφό<ρο>ις ἀνέθηκεν.

In the year of the eponymous archon Dionysodoros, - - sios dedicated me to Phosphoroi.

This stone is reported to be lost.

DEMOKRATIA

12. *Hesperia* 31, 1962, p. 242   333/2 B.C.

[vacat ca. 5 - -] | [ca. 5] ΒΑΣ [ca. 5] vacat ca. 5
[Δη]μοκρατ[ί]α
['Η βουλὴ ἡ] ἐπὶ Νικοκράτους ἄ[ρ]χοντος
[ἀνέθηκ]εν στεφανωθεῖσα ὑπ[ὸ] τοῦ δήμου
[ἀρετ]ῆς ἔνεκα καὶ δικ[αι]οσύνης·

Demokratia
The members of the boule in the year of archon
eponymous Nikokrates
Dedicated it after being crowned by the people
For their virtue and justice.

This important cult of Democracy personified was located in the Agora in Kerameikos near the statues of Harmodios and Aristogeiton (cf. WT. 264). The restored text of the dedicatory inscription on the base of the statue of Demokratia is possible due to the brilliant combination by A. E. Raubitschek of the text in IG, II², 2791 (copied by Fourmont in the church of Vlassarou, stone lost) with a fragment of inscription now in the Epigraphical Museum of Athens (EM. 3913).

Wycherley notes (WT. 696), "Where the statue stood is not known," in the commentary of the text which states that the equestrian statue of King Demetrios had to be erected *"in the Agora, by the statue of Demokratia,"* ignoring also what was said in his own testimonium (WT. 264) from Diodorus Siculus, XX, 46, 2 where is copied the part of the original Athenian decree honoring King Demetrios proposed in 307 B.C. by the orator Stratokles, son of Euthydemos of Diomeia. This document was possibly copied by Diodorus from the collection of decrees by Krateros.

For a complete study of the cult and the literary, epigraphical and artistic testimonia connected with it see A. E. Raubitschek "Demokratia" in *Hesperia* 31. 1962, pp. 238-243, and especially the notes 26 and 27 on p. 241.

58 THE TWO AGORAS

DIONYSOS (Melpomenos?)

13. IG. II², 3479   end of 2nd c. B.C.

Πλείσταινον Σωκλέους Κεφαλῆθεν | Ἡ γυνὴ Πλεῖστις καὶ ἡ θυγάτηρ Σωσινίκη | ἄρχοντα γενόμενον Διονύσωι ἀνέθηκαν.

(statue of) Pleistainos, son of Sokles of Kephale, dedicated to Dionysos by his wife Pleistis and his daughter Sosinike when he was elected archon.

Inscription on a marble base found in the church of Demetrius Katiphoris.

14. IG. II², 3114   end of 1st c. A.D.

Ὁ Δῆμος ἐνείκα
Λούκιος Φλάουιος Φλάμμας
Κυδαθηναιεὺς ἦρχε.
Πάντες χοραγοὶ πᾶς τε φυλέτας χορὸς
ἄγαλμα Δήμωι Κέκροπος ἐστάσαντο με κ.λ.π.

The deme got the prize
In the year of Lucius Flamma of Kydathenaion
as Archon eponymous.
All the sponsors (choreges) and all the
members of the tribe's chorus set up this
dedication to the deme of Cecrops ...etc.

Found in the excavations of the Greek Archaeological Society in the "Stoa Giganton" (Odeion) and later brought to the stoa of Attalos. Marble triangular base for a tripod. For a statue of Dionysos in the Odeion cf. Paus. I. 14, 1 (WT. 2. 521).

DIOSKOURI
(WT. pp. 61-65; T. 133-151)

15. IG. II² 4641   4th c. B.C.

[- - - - ἐ]κ Κοίλης | ['Ανά]κοιν.

(- -, - -) *from the deme of Koile (dedicated.) to the Dioskouri.*

Koehler proposes (in IG. II², 1552 b.) the restoration [τοῖν θε]οῖν. On the stone (marble base) the K is obvious.

ELEOS

Cf. Zeus Agoraios.

ELEUSINION

(WT. pp. 74-85; T. 191-228)

16. Lysias, VI (*Andocides*), 52   soon after 399 B.C.

εἰσελήληθεν ἡμῶν εἰς τὴν πόλιν, καὶ ἔθυσεν ἐπὶ τῶν βωμῶν ὧν οὐκ ἐξῆν αὐτῷ καὶ ἀπήντα τοῖς ἱεροῖς περὶ ἅ ἠσέβησεν, εἰσῆλθεν εἰς τὸ Ἐλευσίνιον, ἐχερνίψατο ἐκ τῆς ἱερᾶς χέρνιβος,...

...*he has entered into our city; he has sacrificed on the altars which were forbidden to him, and has come into the presence of the sanctuaries against which he committed his impiety. He has entered into the Eleusinion and immersed his hands in the sacred basin.* (cf. WT. 714).

Wycherley uses as T. 197 the passage 4 of the same speech. The χέρνιψ of the Eleusinion is known only from this reference.

17. Eupolis, *Demoi.* Fr. 3   5th c. B.C.

[ΣΥ. .....]ος ποτ' εἰς ἀγο[ρὰ]ν κυκεῶ πιὼν
ἐξῆλθε κρ]ίμνων τὴ[ν] ὑπήνην ἀνάπλεως
μυστηρικ]ῶν· τοῦτ' ἐννοοῦμαί πως ἐγώ·
ἐλ]θὼν δὲ ταχέως οἴκαδ' εὐθὺς τοῦ ξένου,
τί] ἔδρασας, ὦ πανοῦργε καὶ κυβευτὰ σύ;
ἔφ]ην, κελεύων τὸν ξένον μοι χρυσίου
δοῦν]αι στατ[ῆ]ρας ἑκατόν· ἦν γὰρ πλούσιος.
χόνδ]ρον (τότ' οὖν) ἐκ[έ]λευσέ μ' εἰπεῖν ὅτι πιὼν
ἐξῆλθεν· εἶτα,] κᾆτ' ἔλαβον τὸ χρυσίον.
διδοὺς δὲ ποι]είτω τὶς γ' ὅ τι ποτε βούλεται.

SYC. ...came into the agora. He had been drinking the Sacred Soup (kykeon). His beard was full of ritual barley-

crumbs. I happened to notice it, and hurried to his home, and went straight up to the stranger, and asked what he had been up to, the dirty cheat. I told him to hand over one hundred staters (2000 drachmas). (He had plenty of money.) So then he urged me to say that it was ordinary gruel that he had been drinking when he came out. So I said it, and got the cash. I don't care what a man does when he pays up.

This story told by a sycophant is connected with the Eleusinion in the Agora. If the ''kykeon'' was not the one connected with the mysteries of the goddesses and if the punishment for a foreigner participating in the ritual were not a severe one, the case could not have been worth 2000 drachmas to be covered up and forgotten by the blackmailer. For the scenic background of the *Demoi* we definitely know that most of the preserved parts at least were set in the city of Athens. In another fragment the blackmailer screams, having been arrested in the Agora, and Aristeides orders the archers to take him to ''Oineus.'' Was the ''kyphon'' (pillory) by the statue of Oineus? (cf. TA. 96-106).

(*DEDICATIONS*)

18. IG. II², 3648   3rd-2nd c. B.C.

[- - - | ἱέρειαν Δήμητρος] καὶ Κόρης
[- - -   - -] ἀνέθηκεν
[ὁ δεῖνα ἐποίη]σεν

(- -, *priestess of Demeter) and Kore (name, patronym, demothen) dedicated... (Sculptor's name) made it.*

From a piece of Pentelic marble (base?) found ''east of Areopagus.''

19. IG. II², 3529   1st c. A.D.

Κλεομένης Μαντίου Μαραθών[ι] | ος καὶ Φιλητὼ Λευκίου
Πειραιέως θυ[γάτηρ] | τὴν ἑαυτῶν θυγατέρα Φιλητὼ μνη |
θεῖσαν ἀφ᾽ [ἑστίας]· Δήμητρι καὶ Κόρῃ

Kleomenes, son of Mantias of Marathon and Phileto,
daughter of Leukios of Piraeus (dedicated this statue of)
their daughter Phileto initiated (into the mysteries) in
the family, to Demeter and Kore.

"Athenis in templo Panagias." It is possible that this
"Panagia" is Vlassarou (cf. TA. 20).

20. IG. II², 3849   4th-3rd c. B.C.?

. . . οδημος [-(father's) n. - deme n. -]
Μένιππον [-(father's) n. - deme n. -]
Δήμητρι καὶ [Κόρηι - - ἀνέθηκεν]

. . .*odemos (son of - - of - -) dedicated (a statue of)*
Menippos. (son of - - of - -) to Demeter and Kore.

This stone was "east of the Hephaisteion (the so-called
Theseion) in the church of Vlassarou." The text has been
edited according to my restoration.

21. IG. II², 4025   middle 4th c. B.C.

Δήμητρι καὶ κόρει | Φίλυ[λ]λα | Φιλοκλέ[ο]υς | Σουνιέ[ω]ς |
θυγάτ[ηρ]. | ['Η Μήτ]ηρ Φιλία 'Α[νέθ]ηκεν. |
Κηφισόδοτος ἐ[π]ο[ί]ησεν.

To Demeter and Kore. (Statue of) Philylla, daughter of
Philokles of Sounion, dedicated by her mother Philia. Ke-
phisodotos made it.

Marble statue base once in the tower of the Winds, now in
the Epigraphical Museum (10034).

22. IG. II², 4640   4th c. B.C.

Μνησικλῆς 'Επικράτου Ο[ἰναῖος - - - - 'Α]μφιτρ[οπ]ῆθεν
Δήμητρι καὶ Κόρη[ι - - - ἀνέθηκαν].

Mnesikles, son of Epikrates of Oinai (name, patronym) of
Amphitrope (...dedicated.) to Demeter and Kore...

A marble epistylium found on the Acropolis and especially
interesting for the architectural study of the temple.

23. IG. II², 4662   4th-3rd c. B.C.?

Δήμητρι.

To Demeter.

A marble base of a dedication found by Kavvadias (*Arch. Eph.* 1898, 14, No. 7) in one of the houses of Apollonos Street.

24. IG. II², 4571   1st-2nd c. A.D.

Πολύτει | μος | Πλούτωνι καὶ Κό | [ρ]ῃ εὐχα | ριστήρι | ον
ἐαυ | τὸν | Εὐχα | ρίστη | ᾽Α[ν]έ | [ϑ]ηκεν.

Polyteimos, to Plouto and Kore in thanksgiving. Euchariste dedicated (an image of himself?).

"Athenis" relief seen by Fourmont.

25. *Hesperia* 29, 1960, p. 37, No. 45   4th c. B.C.

[οἱ? - - ο]ι καὶ οἱ στ[ρατηγοί? - -]
[Δήμητρ]ι καὶ Κόρῃ[ι - - - -]
[ὰ]   ν έ [ϑ η κ α ν]

*[the - -] and the generals (?) dedicated
to Demeter and Kore - - - -*

This inscription on a block of Pentelic marble is possibly a fragment of a statue base. It was found "west of the south end of the stoa of Attalos" in 1937.

26. *Hesperia* 29, 1960, p. 40, No. 50   ca. middle 3rd c. B.C.

[ἐπὶ - -]ου ἄρχοντος [- -]
[- - .] περὶ τὼ θεὼ ἀρ[ήτευε - -]
[- - .]υ ᾽Ασκληπιαδ [- -]
[- - . . .]νιων[- -]
5   [- - . . . . .]ΙΛ[- -]

*[The year of - - name - - as eponymous] archon - - when
- - name - - was ordained for the cult of the two goddesses
- - Asklepiad[es? - -*

Possibly a fragment from a stele of a 'lex sacra,' connected with the Eleusinion, in the area of which the stone was found in 1936.

EPONYMOI

(WT. pp. 85-90; T. 229-245)

27. Schol. Aristophanes, *Peace*, 1183-4

1) Εἷς ἐστὶ τῶν ιϛ' ἀνδριάντων ἐν οἷς ἐγράφοντο οἱ στρατιωτικοὶ κατάλογοι καὶ τὰ κηρύγματα.

2) Ἑκάστης φυλῆς ἐπώνυμος ἦν ἀνδριὰς τοῦ τῶν φυλῶν ἐξηγησαμένου, Αἰαντίδος, Οἰνηίδος, Ἀκαμαντίδος καὶ τῶν λοιπῶν, ἔνθα ἐτίθεντο τὰ ὀνόματα τῶν ἐπ' ἐξόδῳ καταλελεγμένων.

3) Τόπος Ἀθήνησιν παρὰ πρυτανεῖον ἐν ὧι ἑστήκασι ἀνδριάντες, οὓς ἐπωνύμους καλοῦσιν. Ἐπειδὰν οὖν κατάλογον δεήσῃ γενέσθαι στρατείας, προσγράφοντες τὰ ὀνόματα τῶν καταλεγομένων ἐπὶ ἑνὸς προτιθέασι τούτων τῶν ἀνδριάντων, ὑπὲρ τοῦ φανερὸν ἐκεῖσε γενέσθαι τοῖς καταλεγομένοις.

1) *One of the twelve statues on which the military enlistments and summons were written.*

2) *For each tribe (Aiantis, Oineis, Akamantis and the others) was a statue of the hero who was elected as ancestral leader. (In the place where those statues stood) the names of the citizens enlisted for the expedition were displayed for the public.*

3) *The place in Athens, close to the Prytaneion, where statues stood of those (heroes) who are called eponymoi. So, whenever there is a need for enlisting for an expedition (the archons) write the names of those who are elected for enlistment in columns, one by one, and they display them in public before those statues so that those who are called to arms will know.*

Wycherley uses as T. 232 the text of Aristophanes, but uses only part of the scholiast's note in his commentary. The three scholia are very useful in understanding the topogra-

phy of the Agora. For the epithet "Archegetai" used for
the eponyms cf. TA. 33.

28. Aristotle, Ath. Pol., 21, 6   ca. 329-322 B.C.

Ταῖς δὲ φυλαῖς ἐποίησεν ἐπωνύμους ἐκ τῶν προκριθέντων
ἑκατὸν ἀρχηγετῶν, οὓς ἀνεῖλεν ἡ Πυθία δέκα.

*He called each tribe by the name of a founding-hero. The
ten were chosen by the Pythia from a list of one hundred
chief (Attic) heroes.*

For texts mentioning the chief heroes, cf. TA 33 under
Twelve Gods.

HARMODIOS AND ARISTOGEITON
(WT. pp. 93-98; T. 256-280)

29. Papyrus Berolini, 13045, Fr. ii, lines 315-18 3rd c. A.D.

Ἐσ[τι δὲ] θάνα[τος ἡ κε]ιμένη κρίσις τοῖς τ[υ]ράννοις
Ἁρμόδι[ος οὐ μὴν φόνου φεύγει] | [ὁ] ταῦτ[α δ]ιαπε[πραγ-
μένος] ἀλλὰ κατὰ τὴν | ἀγορὰν ἔ[σ]τηκε [πα]ρ[ώ]ν, μετὰ
χεῖρας ἔχων | τὸ ξίφος, προβεβλημένος, γυμνός·....

*Death is the accepted punishment for tyrants. Harmodios,
the one who exacted this order of the law, does not flee for
having murdered, but here in the Agora he stands, present
to all, holding in his hands the sword, advancing forward,
nude...*

This is the unique text which, referring to the statues of
the Tyrannicides, gives the description of the statue of Harmodios.

30. Isaios, V. (*Dikaiogenes*), 47   420-350 B.C.

καὶ ἐβουλήθης μᾶλλον Δικαιογένους καλεῖσθαι υἱὸς ἢ Ἁρμοδίου, ὑπεριδὼν μὲν τὴν ἐν Πρυτανείῳ σίτησιν, καταφρονή-
σας δὲ προεδριῶν καὶ ἀτελειῶν, ἅ τοῖς ἐξ ἐκείνων γεγονόσι
δέδοται

...and you preferred to be called son of Dikaiogenes rather than a descendant of Harmodios, considering valueless the meals in the Prytaneion, and thinking nothing of the presidencies and the tax exemptions which are given to those who descend in line from those (two) men.

The text mentions the honors given to descendants of the Tyrannicides, sometimes connected with the epigraphical material of the Agora.

31. Hypereides, *Against Philippides*, 3   ca. 336 B.C.

ἔπειθ' ὅτι ἐν νόμῳ γράψας ὁ δῆμος ἀπεῖπεν μήτε λέγειν ἐξεῖναι μηδενὶ κακῶς ʿΑρμόδιον καὶ ʾΑριστογείτονα μήτ' ἆσαι ἐπὶ τὰ κακίονα.

And secondly because the people drew up a law forbidding anyone to speak ill of Harmodios and Aristogeiton or to make parodies of the songs about them.

The law mentioned in this passage was probably a decree inscribed on a stele, possibly one standing close to the statues.

HEPHAISTOS
(WT. pp. 98-102; T. 281-295)

32. Harpokration   1st.-2nd c. A.D.

Χαλκεῖα/ʿΥπερείδης ἐν τῷ κατὰ Δημέου ξενίας. Τὰ Χαλκεῖα ἑορτὴ παρ' ʾΑθηναίοις ἀγομένη Πυανεψιῶνος ἔνῃ καὶ νέᾳ, χειρώναξι κοινή, μάλιστα δὲ χαλκεῦσιν, ὥς φησιν ʾΑπολλώνιος ὁ ʾΑχαρνεύς. Φανόδημος δὲ οὐκ ʾΑθηνᾷ φησιν ἄγεσθαι τὴν ἑορτὴν ἀλλ' ʿΗφαίστῳ. Γέγραπται δὲ καὶ Μενάνδρῳ δρᾶμα Χαλκεῖα.

Coppersmiths' festival: mentioned by Hypereides in the speech "Against Demeas, for Usurping Citizens' Rights." The Coppersmiths' Feast is an Athenian holiday celebrated the first day of the month Pyanepsion, common to all laborers, but especially to coppersmiths, according to Apollonios of Acharnai. Phanodemos (the Atthido-

grapher) *says that the holiday is not to honor Athena but Hephaistos. Menander wrote a comedy called "The Coppersmiths' feast."*

For the date of the "Coppersmiths' feast" Harpokration refers to a lost treatise written by Apollonios of Acharnai. The mention of both Athena and Hephaistos in the discussion of the festival reminds one of their common cult in the Hephaisteion. The festival was celebrated by the bronze-workers and the other laborers and we know that at least several "Unions" had their trade center around the hill of Agoraios Kolonos. Among the laborers we must include the "Kolonetai" or hired men. For the hired men cf. Harpokraion, *Kolonetas* (WT. 286) and for the coppersmiths cf. Andokides, I, 40; Bekker, Anecd. Gr. I, 316, 23; *Hesperia,* VII, 1938, p. 339.

HERA BOULAIA

33. IG. II², 4675   middle 3rd c. B.C.

῞Ηραι Βουλαίαι
['Α]πο[λ]λό[δ]ωρος 'Αρίστωνος: 'Ο[ῆθεν]
[Π ρ]οστάξαντος τοῦ θεοῦ ἀν[έθηκεν]
'Επ[ὶ] 'Ι[ε]ρ[έως] Κηφισοφῶντος
'Αθμ[ον]έ[ως] τὸ πέντττον.

To Hera Boulaia

Apollodoros, son of Ariston of Oe
As ordered by the god, dedicated it.

When Kephisiphon of Athmonon
Was priest for the fifth year.

From a stele of Hymmetian marble. Kephisophon from Athmonon, "priest for the fifth year," seems like the priest of Zeus Boulaios. This is the unique mention of the cult.

HERAKLES

In Pausanias I. 8, 4 (WT. 117) it is mentioned that a statue of Herakles stood *"by the temple of Ares"* with statues of Theseus and Apollo. We do not know that this statue was there for cult purposes, yet we may suppose so for there is no other place in the Agora area for his cult.

The temple of Ares is the closest temple to the altar of the Twelve Gods and according to a restored passage of the speech "Against Demosthenes" by Hypereides (fr. vii. xxxii, 2-5) the Athenians were obliged to erect a statue of Alexander the Great as the *"Thirteenth God"* (cf. Aelian, *Varia Historia*, V. 12). This statue of the deified king in the Agora was probably of the same type and was like the cult statue of his shrine in the gymnasium of Kynosarges (cf. *Archeion Pontou*, XXII, 1958, pp. 240-242). This new god was called "Herakles Dionysos" (the type that archaeologists call the youthful Herakles) and we know that a head of such a statue was found near the Agora area (Nat. Arch. Mus. in Athens, No 366.) (Cf. M. Bieber, *Alexander the Great in Greek and Roman Art*, 1964).

34. An ephebic list on a herm found in the church of Demetrios Katiphoris (IG. II², 3744 "Aet. imp.") is offered by the donors to *"Herakles Leontas"* and *"Herakles Alexandros."*

...Ἡρακλῆι Λεοντᾶι... Ἡρακλῆι Ἀλεξάνδρωι

This is the unique epigraphical evidence of the deification of Alexander the Great as Herakles and has never previously beeen used in connection with the discussion of his deification in the city of Athens.

THEMIS BOULAIA

35. Plutarch, *Praec. Ger. Reip.*, 802b   ca. 46 - ca. 120 A.D,

Ὁ δὲ τῆς Πολιάδος Ἀθηνᾶς καὶ τῆς Βουλαίας Θέμιδος..

The spokesman for Athena Polias and Themis Boulaia.

According to Plutarch, Athena Polias and Themis Boulaia had the same symbolism. This passage is the unique mention of this cult.

THESEUS
(WT. pp. 115-119; T. 339-362)
(TA. XXIX-XXXIV)

36. Plutarch, *Theseus*, 4, I   ca. 46 - ca. 120 A.D.

Σιλανίωνα τιμῶσι καὶ Παρράσιον, εἰκόνων Θησέως γραφεῖς καὶ πλάστας γενομένους.

They honor Silanion and Parrhassius who were sculptors and painters of images of Theseus.

For a comparison of the painting of Theseus by Parrhasius with that by Euphranor, cf. Plutarch, *De Gloria Atheniensium*, 2 (TA. 4). Another Theseus painted by Parrhasius is mentioned in Pliny (N. H. XXXV. 69) that *"Romae in Capitolio fuit."*

In Synesios, *Epist.*, 54 we read that *"the proconsul took away the painted boards from the Poikile."* It is not impossible that the *"portable painting"* in the Capitolium was once in one of the Agora buildings.

Silanion was a famous Athenian sculptor and from this passage of Plutarch we learn that he made *"statues of Theseus."* Perhaps these are connected with the "Temenos" or the "Shrine" of Theseus in the city of Athens.

37. Schol. Aeschines, III (Ktesiphon) 13, a

Ἀποκληροῦσιν· ἀντὶ τοῦ διὰ κλήρου παρέχουσιν τὴν ἀρχὴν ἐν τῷ Θησείῳ, ἴσως τῶν θεσμοθετῶν ἐκεῖ ἀεὶ χειροτονούντων εὐτελεῖς τινας διοικήσεις, ὡς πρὸς τιμὴν τοῦ Θησέως τοῦ οἰκιστοῦ, Οὗτινος τὰ ὀστᾶ ἐκεῖ ἔκειτο. Νόμος δ᾽ ἦν τοὺς ἀποφυγόντας τῶν οἰκετῶν εἰς τὸ τοῦ Θησέως τέμενος ἀτιμωρήτους εἶναι.

They draw lots: Instead of allotting magistracies in the Theseion, perhaps because the Thesmothetai always elect some minor magistracies there to honor Theseus the settler whose remains were buried there. It was also the law that those escaped slaves who sought asylum in the temenos of Theseus could not be punished.

The scholiast clearly distinguishes between the "Shrine" of Theseus (Theseion) and the sacred precinct (Temenos). This text helps in the restoration of the following scholium which gives specific information about the cult of the Athenian hero (cf. TA. 30).

38. Schol. Aeschines, III (Ktesiphon), 13, b

Δύο Θησεῖα· ἐν τῇ πόλει <τέμενος Θησέως, Κίμωνος> αὐτοῦ ἐπιτάφιον ποιήσαντος· καὶ ἔξω τῆς πόλεως, ὃ ἔκτισεν αὐτῷ ἱερόν, ὅτε κατένεγκεν αὐτοῦ ἐκ Σκύρου τὰ ὀστᾶ.

Two Theseia, a (sacred precinct) in the "old city" established (by Kimon) on his (Theseus') grave and a shrine outside the boundaries of the old city also erected by Kimon when he brought the remains of Theseus from the island of Skyros.

The key to the correct interpretation and restoration of the text is in the meaning of the word πολις which in this case follows the old tradition of the topographical term *"old town."* According to Thucydides, II, 15, the Acropolis and the area before the south slope were the old town and the scholion says that the one "Theseion" where Theseus' remains were buried was there, and the other "outside the old town."

The Theseion in the "old town" is well known from many references. It was near the Aglaureion (thus in the area of the ancient Agora) and the shrine of the "Semnai theai" (the Erinyes). The Propylon of the Acropolis was not far. The "Temenos" was a recognized sanctuary for slaves. Three boundary stones have been found thus far; one in the Odeion of Herodes (IG, I², 860), one on the south slope (IG, I², 861), and one in the house of Finlay close to the church of St. Andrew (IG, I², 862).

Literary testimonia for the Theseion in the "old town" are: Aristophanes, *Knights*, 1311-12 and Schol. (WT. 341, 342), Aristotle, *Const. of Athens*, 15, 4 (WT. 344). Diodorus

Siculus, IV, 62, 4 (WT. 384) and WT. 346, 349, 350, 352, 357, 358, 360.

For the accuracy of this interpretation cf. Thucydides VI, 61, 2 where the "Theseion in the old town" is mentioned.

As for the hero shrine of Theseus (Theseion) "outside the old town," Plutarch says that it was "in the middle of the city beside the present gymnasium" (*Theseus*, 36, 2; WT. 356) and agreement can be found in Pausanias (I. 17, 2-3; WT. 351). Close to this shrine was located a school and the "Shrine" of the hero physician (Demosth., XVIII, 129).

39. IG. II², 4763   2nd. c. A.D.?

Θησέως.

Theseus

The inscription is carved on the left foot of a statue which once stood on a base No. 2815 of the Epigraphical Museum.

TWELVE GODS
(WT. pp. 119-122. T. 363-378)

40. SEG. XVI, 172   Middle 4th c. B.C.

[- -]ρικὸ | [- -]εὺς | [Δώδεκα ϑ]εοῖς
[- - - ἐπο]ίησεν

(*name, son of - -*) *rikos of - -* , (*to the Twelve G*)*ods.*
(*Sculptor's name*) *made it.*

A marble base found in the Agora and later brought to the Roman Market.

The Altar of the Twelve Gods was always known in Athens by this name and both epigraphical and literary testimonia give evidence of its existence until the second century A.D. (cf. IG, II², 5065; Plutarch, *Vit. X Orat.*, 847a. WT, 377, 698). The passage of Plutarch can not be based on a text dated before the year 280 B.C. when the degree proposed by Demochares for a statue of Demosthenes was voted by the boule (cf. "Neon Athenaion," I, 1955, pp. 195ff).

ARCHAGETAI GODS

41. Hesychios, *Archagetai*   5th c. A.D.

Ἀρχαγέται, ἥρωες ἐπώνυμοι τῶν φυλῶν, ἢ θεοὶ ἐν Ἀθήναις.

*Archagetai, heroes eponymous of the tribes or gods in
Athens.*

The "ἀρχαγέται" can hardly be anything other than
the Twelve Gods of the twelve Attic cities which took part
in the new settlement of Athens by Theseus. The common
altar of these gods stood in the center of the city as a symbol
of the union and the hero-shrine of Theseus was here (cf.
Theseus.)

Philochoros (in Strabo, IX, 20. 597a) names eleven of these
cities as follows: *"Kekropia, Tetrapolis, Epakria, Dekeleia,
Aphidna, Eleusis, Thorikos, Brauron, Kytherros, Sphettos* and
Kephissia." The twelfth city of the "Dodekapolis" was
"Tetrakomon," according to Loeper, for Arvanitopoulos
"Aixone," but it is also possible that it was *"Phaleron,"*
"Phyle" or *"Araphen."*

It may also be that the *"eponymous gods"* were the Eponymous of the twelve Attic "tribes" which existed before
the Kleistheneian tribes (Aristotle, *Const. of Athens,* 21, 3.)

ZEUS AGORAIOS
(WT. pp. 122-124; T. 379-386)

The altar of Zeus Agoraios in the Agora is the "Altar
of Pity" (Eleos) mentioned by Pausanias (I. 17, 1., WT.
177). "Agoraios" is a local epithet for the cult of Zeus
Meilichios (WT. p. 124) introduced by Theseus in the
"Old Town Agora." (For these identifications see above
TA. XXXV-XL).

The Altar of Zeus Agoraios-Meilichios of the Ancient Agora is also mentioned by Aeschylus, *Eumenides,* lines 973-975
(WT. 379) wherein it is clear that the altar stood between

the Acropolis (cult of Athena) and Areopagus (cult of the Erinyes).

Four inscribed dedications to Zeus Meilichios were found in the Agora excavations (mentioned in WT. p. 124), but their evidence was not enough to convince Wycherley of the existence of a cult of the chthonic Attic Zeus in the later marketplace of Athens. After the discovery of two more dedications (cf. TA. XXXIX, XL) in the Agora "in the old town" and the identification of the cult of Meilichios-Eleos with Zeus Agoraios, the two dedications discovered earlier on the north slope of the hill of the Nymphs (IG, II², 4677, 4678) must be attributed to one of the two known locations for the cult.

42. *Hesperia* 12, 1943, pp. 48-51, No 9   4th c. B.C.

"Ολυμπος | Διὶ Μιλιχίωι

Olympos to Zeus Meilichios

43. *Hesperia,* ibidem, No. 10   4th c. B.C.

Διὶ Μ<ι>λ[ιχίωι] | 'Αριστο[- -] | καὶ Φιλακ[ὼ - τοδ'].
ἀνέσ [τησαν]

To Zeus Meilichios Aristo - - and Philako [set up this].

44. *Hesperia* ibidem, No 11   4th c. B.C.

[Διὶ Μιλι]χίωι | [-ca. 6-]ιος

To Zeus Meilichios, ---ios.   ..

45. *Hesperia* 21, 1952, p. 377, No. 33   4th c. B.C.

Θεοδ[- - - Διὶ Μιλιχίωι]

Theod - - -(to Zeus Meilichios).

The restoration of lines 3-4 in TA. 43 appears more probable to me than ἀν<έϑ>εσ[αν]. In 45 the restoration of the name and epithet of the god is supported by the preserved part of the relief with a bearded snake.

ZEUS PHRATRIOS

46. IG. II², 4975   4th c. B.C.

'Ιερὰ Διὸς | Φρατρίο[υ] | καὶ 'Αθηνᾶ[ς].

Sacred to Zeus Phratrios and Athena.

Found in the excavations of the Greek Archaeological Society in the stoa of Attalos. The inscription is in the Epigraphical Museum, 620. For inscriptions found later in the Agora area see WT. p. 52, T. 112.

ZEUS STRATIOS

47. IG. II², 4723   1st c. A.D.

'Αγαθῆ Τύχη | [Διὶ] Στρατίῳ |
[Πολ]έμων κα[ὶ] [Δομ]ετιανὸς | [Γερμ]ανικοπο |
[λῖτα]ι καὶ Α[... | .... εὐ]χῆς χ[άριν] |

Good Fortune/To Zeus Stratios
Polemon and Dometianus of Germanikopolis
and A - - (dedicated me) wishing the blessing of God.

Base of an altar found near the church of Panagia Vlassarou. For the cult of Zeus Stratios cf. IG. II², 4739, 4785.

ZEUS BOULAIOS

Cf. Hera Boulaia.

PUBLIC BUILDINGS AND OFFICES
ARCHEIA

48. IG. II², 687 (Dittb., Syll.³ 43/5). lines 44-45   280 B.C.

[ὀμόσαι δὲ] τὰ | ἀρχεῖα τοῖς πρέσβεσιν τοῖς παραγεγο[νόσιν παρ' αὐτῶν].

The ambassadors who came from them must take an oath in the public buildings.

The embassies of the allies took the oath εἰς τὰ ἀρχεῖα. Cf. *Strategion.*

49. Hypereides, (In Defense of Lycophron Fr. III, a—Pollux
IX, 156) 4th c. B.C.

ἢ νεωρίων προδοσίαν ἢ ἀρχείων ἐμπυρισμὸν ἢ κατάληψιν
ἄκρας...

...*either the betrayal of dockyards, the arson of public
administration buildings, or the seizure of the citadel...*

BOULEUTERION

50. Lysias, XX. (In Defense of Polystratos), 14 411 B.C.

ἐπεὶ δὲ ἠναγκάσθη καὶ ὤμοσε τὸν ὅρκον, ὀκτὼ ἡμέρας εἰ-
σελθὼν εἰς τὸ βουλευτήριον ἐξέπλει εἰς Ἐρέτριαν. Καὶ οὗτος
μεν οὔτ᾽ εἰπὼν γνώμην οὐδεμίαν, οὔτε πλέον ὀκτὼ ἡμερῶν
ἐλθὼν εἰς τὸ βουλευτήριον ὤφλε χρήματα τοσαῦτα· τῶν δὲ εἰ-
πόντων ὑμῖν τἀναντία καὶ διὰ τέλους ἐν τῷ βουλευτηρίῳ ὄν-
των πολλοὶ ἀποφεύγασι.

*When he was thus compelled and had taken the oath,
after having entered the Bouleuterion for only eight days,
he sailed to Eretria..., and this man, who had neither proposed any motion nor even entered the Bouleuterion for
more than eight days...*

This passage is important for it mentions the use of the
Bouleuterion by the Boule of the ''Four Hundred.''

METROON
(WT. pp. 150-160. T. 465-519)

51. Julian, V (To the Mother of the Gods), 186b. 332-363 A.D.

ἐξορίζειν αὐτά..., ὥσπερ Ἀθηναῖοι τὰ ψευδῆ γράμματα τοῦ
Μητρώιου.

*to delete them... exactly as the Athenians did. for the
false documents in the Metroon.*

It is interesting to note that at the time of Julian it was
known that the Athenians tried to remove the false state

documents from the files of the city archives which were kept in the Metroon.

(*Dedications*)

52. IG. II², 3959   after 128/9 A:D.

Ή ἐξ 'Αρείου Πάγου βουλὴ | καὶ ἡ βουλὴ τῶν πεντακοσί-
ων | καὶ ὁ δῆμος "Ατταλον - - | - - ἀνέθηκεν ἐν Μητρώῳ.

*The boule of Areopagus and the boule of the Five
Hundred and the assembly of the people dedicated in the
Metroon (a statue of) Attalos - - | - - .*

Pittakis saw the inscription (marble base?) "west of the
ancient Bouleuterion." A possible restoration is "Ατταλον
['Αττάλου Συπαλλήτιον]." For the formula used cf. IG. II²,
3781.

53. IG. II², 4595   328/7 B.C.

Ἱερεὺς Μητρὸς θεῶν "Αρμενος | 'Αντιφάτους : Παμβωτά-
δης ἀνέθη| κε ἐπ' Εὐθυκρίτου ἄρχοντος.

*Priest of the Mother of the Gods, Harmenos son of Anti-
fates of Pambotadae, dedicated, in the year of the eponymous archon Euthykritos.*

A marble base found in the Agora. Epigraphical Museum,
471.

METROON ON THE MUSEUM HILL

54. Arch. Ephemeris, 1899, pp. 239-240   4th c. B.C.

[Ἱι]ερὸν | Μητρός.

Sacred to the Mother (of the Gods).

This inscription is carved on the rock of the Museum Hill
and definitely indicates that a cult of the Mother of the
Gods existed there. Thus the two tiles found on the
Museum Hill (WT. 514) are not connected with the Metroon
of the Agora, but with the "Metroon" of the Museum Hill,
and their inscriptions cannot be included in the testimonia
for the building in the Agora. This second "Metroon" on

the Museum Hill in which the "Dikasterion" (correct in
Apostolios, XI, 34) was established on the tomb of the
"Metragyrtes" has been identified by A. Papagiannopoulos
(Anc. Gr. Inscr., I, pp. 76-77, Athens, 1939) with the site
on the Museum Hill where seven seats are carved in the
rock and traces of the filled pit (barathron) can be seen near
the rock which bears the above inscription.

The text of Photios (s.v. Metragyrtes, WT. 487) as well
as Suidas (s.v. Barathron) shows confusion in the matter of
the "Dikasterion" on the Museum Hill and the Metroon in
the Agora.

ODEION
(WT. pp. 161-162; T. 520-523)

55. Strabo, IX, 1, 17 (396). WT. 91   1st. c. b.c.

ὁμοίως δὲ καὶ ἡ Ἀκαδημία καὶ οἱ κῆποι τῶν φιλοσόφων καὶ
τὸ Ὠδεῖον καὶ ἡ Ποικίλη στοὰ καὶ τὰ ἱερὰ τὰ ἐν τῇ πό|λει
θαυμαστὰ | ἔχοντα τεχνιτῶν ἔργα.

*And in like manner the Academy (grove of the hero
Academus) and the gardens of the philosophers, and the
Odeion, and the Poikile (painted) Stoa, and the sanctuaries
on the Acropolis which possess admirable masterpieces.*

The passage is used by Wycherley for the mention of the
Poikile stoa because he believes that the Odeion is the Periclean. There is no doubt that the Periclean Odeion had been
reconstructed by Ariobarzanes when Strabo wrote this, but
it was not "The Odeion" of Athens (Pausanias calls it "a
structure" and not an Odeion in I. 20, 4) worthy of mention
as a famous building. Jahn and Michaelis in *Arx Athenarum*
do not include Strabo's passage among the testimonia of the
Periclean Odeion.

The short text of Hesychios (s. v. Odeion) which clearly
belongs to the testimonia of the Periclean Odeion (cf. Jahn-
Michaelis, *Arx Athenarum*, p. 35, 3rd ed. 1901) is used instead by Wycherley as a possible reference to the "orchestra"
in the Agora." (cf. *Orchestra*).

ORCHESTRA
(WT. pp. 162-163; T. 542-528)

The first place called an "orchestra," in use, according to an unknown source used by Eustathius, *on Odyssey*, III, 350. WT. 524, "before the theatre in the shrine of Dionysos was built" (e.g. before the 6th c. B.C.) w a s "in the Agora." But from a comparative study of the testimonia it becomes apparent that it was in the "Old Town Agora" on the south slope of the Acropolis close to the entrance of the fort and below the Nike Tower. Later, in the second century A.D. the Odeion built by Herodes was erected almost in the same place. The "Ikria" (bleachers) were first erected in the early "orchestra" and later were used for early theatrical performances in the nearby shrine of Dionysos when the first orchestra was built there (6th c. B.C.) until the 70th Olympiad (499/6 B.C.) when, during a theatrical contest, they collapsed killing many people in the audience (cf. Suidas, s.v. Pratinas).

The "Poplar" which was "above the theatre" (Eustathius, *on Odyssey*, V, 64) "near which the ikria were (erected by) pounding" and where "those who did not have places watched the show" is not connected with the Agora area, and the imaginary "primitive theatre" in the Agora has been born from misinterpreted texts (cf. WT. 721-723, 725-728 and commentary).

The "ikropoioi (Platform or bleacher-makers), "those who pound (together) the platforms in the Agora area," (Pollux, VII, 125) may also be connected with the seats erected to provide a better view of the processions passing through the Panathenaic Street on great festival days. It is presumed that this was the same procedure followed today in Pasadena, California for the "Rose Bowl Parade." The text of Hegesandros (Athenaeus, IX, 167f) helps to place "the stoa of the Herms" facing the Panathenaic Street in a place between the "Altar of the Twelve Gods" and the Dipylon gates (cf. WT. 302 and 528 for the texts of Pollux and Hegesandros).

56. Timaios Sophistes, *Lexicum Platonicum.* 4th c. A.D.

ὀρχήστρα· τὸ τοῦ θεάτρου μέσον χωρίον, καὶ τόπος ἐπιφανὴς εἰς πανήγυριν, ἔνθα Ἁρμοδίου καὶ Ἀριστογείτονος εἰκόνες.

Orchestra: the central part of the theatre, and also a conspicuous place for a festal gathering, where (are?-were?) the statues of Harmodios and Aristogeiton.

The short and unclear text of Timaios (Lexicum Platonicum, s.v. Orchestra) is the only one in support of the theory that the area where the Odeion and the later stoas were built was called "orchestra." But the date of this text (not earlier than the 4th c. A.D.) and the peculiar syntax without a verb give no evidence of the date when the statues oα the Tyrannicides were in the orchestra. If the omitted verb is εἰσὶν (are), there is a possibility that the statues were in it when Timaios wrote his *Lexicum Platonicum* after the sack of Athens by the Herulians (267 A.D.) and the destruction of the Agora area, and that the statues had been moved *from* the Agora *to* the orchestra (perhaps for protection during the siege). This orchestra, then, might be anywhere in the Athens of the 4th c. A.D. (cf. WT. 276 also quoting Timaios which Wycherley translates "where stood the statues.").

PRYTANEION
(WT. pp. 166-174; T. 541-571)

57. Bekker, *Anecdota Graeca,* I. 242

Ἐπάλξεις: ἐξοχαὶ τειχῶν, προμαχῶνες, ἀψίς. Ἔστι δὲ καὶ δικαστήριον τῶν φονικῶν, ᾠκοδόμηται δὲ πρὸς τῷ Πρυτανείῳ.

Epalxeis: Projections of walls, battlements, apses; "epalxeis" is also the appellation of one of the homicide lawcourts built close to the Prytaneion.

It is clear from the name used for the lawcourt that the building of the Prytaneion was located not far from a city wall. Is this wall the north part of the Pelargikon? Is the law court called "Epalxeis" the same one as "the court at the Prytaneion" (Pollux, VIII, 120; decree in Andocides, I, 78; Demosthenes, XXIII, 76; Pausanias I. 28, 10-11), or another one? For the wall we may only say that the identification with the Pelargikon is supported by two passages of Lucian (*Bis Accusatus*, 9; *Piscator*, 42), the unique evidences to date that the ring of this defense structure on the north side passed around the north slope of the Acropolis (cf. TA. 22, 48 and TA. XXXI).

STRATEGION
(WT. pp. 174-177; T. 572-581)

58. Lysias, IX. (For the Soldier, 4-7   395-386 B.C.

Ἀφικόμενος προπέρυσιν εἰς τὴν πόλιν, οὔπω δύο μῆνας ἐπιδεδημηκὼς κατελέγην στρατιώτης. Αἰσθόμενος δὲ τὸ πραχθὲν ὑπετοπούμην εὐθέως ἐπὶ μηδενὶ ὑγιεῖ κατειλέχθαι. Προσελθὼν οὖν τῷ στρατηγῷ, ἐδήλωσα ὅτι ἐστρατευμένος εἴην, ἔτυχον δὲ οὐδενὸς τῶν μετρίων. Προπηλακιζόμενος δὲ ἠγανάκτουν μὲν ἡσυχίαν δ' εἶχον. Ἀπορούμενος δὲ καὶ συμβουλευόμενός τινι τῶν πολιτῶν τί χρήσωμαι τῷ πράγματι, ἐπυθόμην ὡς καὶ δήσειν με ἀπειλοῖεν λέγοντες ὅτι «οὐδὲν ἐλάττω χρόνον Καλλικράτους Πολύαινος ἐνδημοίη». Κἀμοὶ μὲν τὸ προείρημένα διείλεκτο ἐπὶ τῇ Φιλίου τραπέζῃ· οἱ δὲ μετὰ Κτησικλέους τοῦ ἄρχοντος, ἀπαγγείλαντός τινος ὡς ἐγὼ λοιδοροῦμι, τοῦ νόμου ἀπαγορεύοντος ἐάν τις ἀρχὴν ἐν συνεδρίῳ λοιδορῇ, παρὰ τὸν νόμον ζημιῶσαι ἠξίωσαν.

Τοῦ μὲν νόμου διαρρήδην ἀγορεύοντος τοὺς ἐν τῷ συνεδρίῳ λοιδοροῦντας ζημιοῦν ἀκηκόατε. Ἐγὼ δ' ὅτι μὲν οὐκ εἰσῆλθον εἰς τὸ ἀρχεῖον, μάρτυρας παρεσχόμην,... Εἰ γὰρ φανερός εἰμι μὴ ἐλθὼν εἰς τὸ συνέδριον, ὁ δὲ νόμος τοὺς ἐ ν τ ὸ ς πλημμελοῦντας ἀγορεύει τὴν ζημίαν ὀφείλειν,...

The year before last, when I came back to the city and was in residence less than two complete months, my name appeared on the enlistment rolls as a soldier. When I became aware of what had been done I suspected at once that this enrollment was not a 'clean' one. So I went to

the general (of my tribe) and I declared. that I had al-
ready participated in expeditions, but no courtesy was
shown for my case. Being grossly insulted my temper was
boiling, but I managed to keep quiet. Being at a loss on
what action to take, and when I was trying to consult a
fellow citizen as to how to handle the case, I was informed
that they even threatened to put me in jail, saying, ''Poly-
aenos is back in the city just as long as Kallikrates.'' Now,
what I have just mentioned was said in the bank of Philias
and those of the band of the magistrate Ktesikles, in-
formed by someone that I was swearing, although the law
prohibits swearing only against the holder of a magistracy
at session, tried unlawfully to fine me.

Now you have heard the law clearly stating punishment
for those who swear where a session takes place. I produced
witnesses for the fact that I hadn't even entered the
building where the magistrates' were in session, and the
law states that only those who misbehave inside must pay
a fine,...

The Scholiast of Aristophanes (*Peace* 1183-4, cf. above *E-*
ponymoi) says that the rolls of enlistments and of men chosen
for military services were displayed to the public on the
enclosure of the statues of the Eponymoi. It is clear that
Polyaenos read here that his name was on the roll of an
expeditionary force. Full of fury he immediately went to
the Strategion, but he found no satisfaction from the general
of his tribe and he quarreled with him. After leaving the
Strategion he stopped for a while at the bank of Philias
where he talked with "a citizen" asking for advice. There,
another citizen (who had just left the Strategion) disclosed
to Polyaenos what the general had said about him after he
left. The bank of Philias cannot have been far from the
Strategion as the narration indicates. The "soldier" had
probably spoken of the general in strong terms about his
problem, but in his speech he says he didn't do it "in the
ἀρχεῖον" (Strategion) because there he was "angry, but
quiet." The law, said Polyaenos, penalized only those "who

speak evil in the assembly of the magistrates.'' The word συνέδριον is used in its general sense in this speech as ''the building where magistrates met'' (cf. Pollux, IX, 41).

This text, correctly interpreted, supports the archaeological evidence for the identification of the Strategion with the building in the southwest part of the Tholos. According to the narration of ''the soldier,'' the Strategion is in the Agora not far from the banks or ''tables of the moneylenders,'' and probably also close to the statues of the Eponymoi heroes.

Who were the ''followers of the magistrate Ktesikles'' who fined Polyaenos? We have reference to ''public servants'' whose names are not mentioned because they are slaves, but we are not sure of their superintendant's office. He might have been either one of the five ''Agoranomoi'' or one of the five ''Astynomoi,'' the main magistrates who regulated public behaviour in the Agora. In a decree of 320/19 B.C. (IG. II², 380, lines 15-19) we read that ''the duties of the Astynomoi are imposed on the Agoranomoi,'' so we may suppose that the latter were the regularly elected magistrates sometimes replaced by the former. The Agoranomoi had the right to impose small fines for bad behaviour in the Agora by free citizens and to order the whipping of slaves.

The ''Kyphon'' or the ''Wooden structure'' where the slaves were tied to be whipped was *in the Agora* ''close to the building where the magistrates met'' (=ἀρχεῖον, cf. Suidas; s.v. Kyphon, and below, *Kyphon*), but we don't know if this refers to the ''Agoranomeion'' or to the ''Astynomeion.'' This problem can only be answered by a special study of the Agora inscriptions.

Two recently published inscriptions from the Agora shed more light on the Strategion.

59. *Hesperia* 29, 1960, p. 56, No. 80   early 2nd c. B.C.

[- -]τίου Λεωνίδης
[- - -] ὑπογραμματεὺς
[ἥρωι] στρατηγῶι
[ἀνέθηκεν] vacat

5   [ἐπὶ - - Αἰ]γιλιέως [- -]
     [- - -]ει vacat
     [- -]ϱ[- -]

- - - Leonides (-of name of deme) subsecretary
(dedicated) to the (Hero) Strategos - -
(When name) of Aegilia (- -)

Here for the second time appears a dedication to the Hero
Strategos from the Agora excavations (cf. *Hesperia* 15, 1946,
p. 221 No. 48; WT. p. 176) making it more possible to associate this cult with the Strategion. Perhaps more important
in my judgment is the fact that a minor archon (subsecretary) is the dedicator, inasmuch as we need to identify a
minor archonship connected with the Strategion in order to
understand the office of the "archon Ktesikles" who imposed
the fine on Polyaenos (See TA. 58).

60. *Hesperia* 30, 1961, p. 268, No. 95   early 2nd c. B.C.

     [- - - -]άσιο[ν]
     [ὁ ὑπογραμματεὺς? - -]νη<ς> Θημακ<ε>ὺς
     [καὶ οἱ τεταγμ]ένοι ἐπὶ στρατηγίου
     [- - - καὶ] φι[λοτ]ιμ[ίας ἕνεκεν]
          [- - - -]

- - of the - - deme. (The subsecretary) - nes of
Themakos (and those) placed on guard at the Strategion.
(dedicated this honoring his - - -) and his generosity.
(To - - - - -).

In line 3 of the inscription we read that the dedicators
were "those placed on guard at the Strategion" under the
leadership of an archon whose name appears without patronym exactly as in the previous dedication of almost the
same period by Leonides. This leads us to the suggested restoration of line 2. The question now arises: Are those "placed
on guard at the Strategion" also "those of the band of the
magistrate Ktesikles"? and if so, were they archers or free
citizens?

THOLOS

(Σf. '27,3)

61. Zonaras, *Lexicon*, p. 1047

Θόλος: οἴκημα στρογγυλοειδές. Οὕτως 'Αλέξανδρος.

Tholos: a somewhat circular building, as Alexander (uses it).

This Alexander was the Athenian comic poet, as Meineke points out in FCG, I, p. 486; IV, p. 555.

MARKET

KYKLOI

(WT. pp. 188-190; T. 616-622)

62. Antiphanes, (*Plousioi*)   4th c. B.C.

(Athen., VIII, 342f-343a)

Φοινικίδης δὲ Ταυρέας θ' ὁ φίλτατος,
ἄνδρες παλαιοὶ ὀψοφάγοι τοιοῦτοί τινες,
οἷοι καταβροχθίζειν ἐν ἀγορᾷ τὰ τεμάχη,
ὁρῶντες ἐξέθνησκον ἐπὶ τῷ πράγματι,
ἔφερον δὲ δεινῶς τὴν ἀνοψίαν πάνυ.
κύκλους δὲ συναγείροντες ἔλεγον τοιαδί,
ὡς οὐ βιωτὸν ἐστιν οὐδ' ἀνασχετὸν
τῆς μὲν θαλάσσης ἀντιποιεῖσθαί τινας
ὑμῶν ἀναλίσκειν τε πολλὰ χρήματα,
ὄψου δὲ δεῦρο μηδὲν εἰσπλεῖν μηδὲ γρῦ.
Τί οὖν ὄφελος τῶν νησιάρχων ἐστί; δεῖ
νόμῳ κατακλεῖσαι τοῦτο, παραπομπὴν ποιεῖν
τῶν ἰχθύων.

Phoinikides too, and my friend Taureas,
Such great inveterate epicures that they
would devour all the remnants in the market;
They at this sight seem'd almost like to die,
And bore the scarcity with small good humor;
But gather'd circles around them and spoke to them

"What an intorelable thing it is
That any of you men should claim the sea,
And spend much money in marine pursuits,
While not one fin of fish comes to this market!
What is the use of all our governors
Who sway the islands? We must make a law
That there should be copious importation
Of every kind of fish..."

The description of the "Kykloi" by Antiphanes explains well their meaning for the Athenian citizens' public life in the Agora. The "circles of people" were crowds of citizens standing and talking in the open spaces of the Agora and in the stoas, discussing problems of common interest such as prices of goods, news from other cities and countries, laws, and decrees to be proposed in the Assembly of the people (Ekklesia).

63. Hypereides, *Against Philippides*, 2　　　　ca. 336 B.C.

καὶ Δημοκράτη[ς συν | αὐτ]οῖς ὁ Ἀφιδναῖος [ἀεὶ |
παρ]ακαθήμενος καὶ [κύκ | λ]ον ἱστὰς γελωτοπ[οιεῖ | ἐ]πὶ
τοῖς τῆς πόλεως [δυ]στυχήμασιν καὶ λοι[δορεῖ] θ' ὑμῖν μεθ'
ἡμέρα[ν ἐν | τ]ῆι ἀγορᾶι, εἰς ἑσπέρα[ν δὲ | δε]ιπνήσων
ὡς ὑμ[ᾶς ἐπ | ἐ]ρχεται.

And Demokrates of Aphidna, who never leaves their sides, gathers a circle around him and makes jokes of the city's misfortunes. And he makes fun of you by day in the marketplace but by night comes to dine at the city's honorary table.

This text has been restored after my new readings of the Papyrus (Brit. Mus. 134). This is a description of discussions in a "circle of people." Demokrates of Aphidna, an old politician known for his bitter humor (cf. TA. 48a) used it among "circles" of listeners in the Agora to ridicule the government.

64. Stobaeus, *Anthologium*, XIII, 31   5th c. Λ.D.

Δημοκράτης ἰδὼν κλέπτην ὑπὸ τῶν ἔνδεκα ἀπαγόμενον «'Ά-
θλιε», εἶπε, «τί γὰρ τὰ μικρὰ ἔκλεπτες, ἀλλ' οὐ τὰ μεγάλα, ἵνα
καὶ σὺ ἄλλους ἀπῆγες».

*Demokrates, seeing a thief carried off by the Eleven
cried, "Miserable one, why did you not steal something
grand rather than a trifle? Then you could carry off the
others!"*

This is an example of Demokrates' humor, probably mem-
orized by someone in the "circle" of his audience. We may
presume that the "thief" and the "Eleven" were in the
Agora, and the sarcasm is directed against the financial magistrates of the administration.

BOOTHS
(WT. pp. 190-192; T. 623-627)

65. Oxyrrhynchi Papyrus, 858   2nd-3rd c. A.D.

«Ἐλάτεια γὰρ κατείλημπται», φη | σί, «καὶ πέπαυνται δει-
πνοῦντες οἱ πρυτ[άνεις, | ἀ]νέστησαν δὲ ἐκ τῆς ἀγορᾶς οἱ
τὰς σκ[ηνὰς | ἔ]χοντες, τὸν δὲ σαλπικτὴν μεταπέ[μπε]ταί τις».

*"Elateia is taken," he says,· "the Prytaneis have left
their suppers and the booth traders are being removed from
the market."*

In a fragment of a speech "Against Demosthenes," the
orator (Demades?) attacks what his opponent said in "De
Corona" (XVIII, 169. WT. 623). But his summary is quite
different from the traditional text and it does not mention
τὰ γέρρα (wickerworks).

FISH   ..

66. Aristophanes, (*Nesoi*)   450 B.C.

Ὦ μῶρε μῶρε, ταῦτα παντ' ἐν τῇδ' ἔνι
οἰκεῖν μὲν ἐν ἀγρῷ πρῶτον ἐν τῷ γηδίῳ
ἀπαλλαγέντα τῶν κατ' ἀγορὰν πραγμάτων

καὶ μὴ περιμένειν ἐξ ἀγορᾶς ἰχθύδια
τοιαῦτα, πολυτίμητα, βεβασανισμένα
ἐπ' ἰχθυοπώλου χειρὶ παρανομωτάτῃ.

You fool, you fool! This means one thing:
To live in country peace upon his plot,
Rid of the troubles which lay in the market.

Instead of waiting till the fishlings from the market come,
Like those, paid dear for, and —the sinner—
Squeezed by the hands of the fishmonger.

67. Alexis (*Dorkis*), Fr.i (Athenæus, III, 104) late 4th c. B.C.

Τοῖς ἰχθυοπώλαις ἐστὶν ἐψηφισμένον,
ὥς φασι, χαλκῆν Καλλιμέδοντος εἰκόνα
στῆσαι Παναθηναίησιν ἐν τοῖς ἰχθύσιν
ἔχουσαν ὀπτὸν κάραβον ἐν τῇ δεξιᾷ,

It has been voted by the fish sellers
To set up a bronze statue to Kallimedon
At the Panatheniac festival
In the midst of the fish market; and the statue
Shall, in his right hand, hold a roasted lobster.

GRAIN

68. Dinarchus, (*Against Agasicles*), Fr. vii. (Suidas et Harpocration, s.v. *Prometretes*) 389-322 B.C.

Σκύθου τοίνυν τοῦ προμετρητοῦ ἦν υἱός, ἐν δημοσίοις γέγονε
καὶ αὐτὸς ἐν τῇ ἀγορᾷ προμετρῶν διατετέλεκε καὶ ὑμεῖς ἐκλαμ-
βανόμενοι παρ' αὐτοῦ τοὺς πυροὺς διατελεῖτε.

Moreover he was the son of Skythes the grain measurer,
he has been one of the state's slaves, and he has himself
been a grain measurer up till now in the market, and
you know that because you regularly received the grain
from him.

This fragment of Dinarchus states clearly that grain was counted in the Agora, and it agrees with the decree IG. II², 836 (cf. TA. 1).

Another decree found in the Agora is IG. II², 792 which contains praise for the "Sitonai" (grain buyers) and helps to enlarge our information and knowledge from inscriptions which mention the "Metronomoi (Weight inspectors), "Sitophylakes" (Grain market inspectors), and "Prometretai" (Grain Counters) as being found in the area between the Stoa of Attalos and the west gate of the "Roman Market." (Cf. IG. II², 2886, 3602, 3238; WT. p. 190; Theophrastos, *Characters*, III, 3 "οἱ πυροὶ οἱ ἐν τῇ ἀγορᾷ" ...*the corn in the market*. WT. 7 ff, p. 293.

It seems that the Alphitopolis Stoa was the center of the grain trade (Cf. TA. 1, 2). But it would not be illogical to assume that the other two stoas mentioned by Aristophanes (TA. 1) as being near it, *Stoa Basileios and* "the one by it," used as places for the alleged free public banquets were also somehow connected with the grain trade.

The text of the scholiast of Aristophanes (WT. 8), which was almost rejected by Wycherley who believes that its reference to the Theseion "is no doubt mistaken," (WT. p. 114) and that, "in fact the passage has no connection with the Theseion" (WT. p. 22) becomes one of the most valuable testimonia in the problem of the topography of the Agora in Kerameikos. For this reason the text and its translation are included here.

69. Schol. Aristophanes. *Ecclesiazusae*, 658

ἐς τὴν παρὰ ταύτην τοὺς θῆτας, τοὺς μισθωτοὺς εἰς τὸ Θησεῖον· ἐπεὶ πάλιν ἀπὸ τοῦ θῆτα ἄρχεται.

To the stoa beside this: the Thetes, the hired men, (shall go) to the Theseion; for the first letter of this too is theta.

So, according to the scholiast, the Theseion of the Agora in Kerameikos was either a stoa itself or had a stoa, or perhaps was a building as large and spacious as a stoa which might have then been called one. If the scholiast was correct, and we have no valid reason to doubt that he may have known more of ancient topography of Athens than do modern scholars (cf. TA. 30), the Theseion was located in the same area as the Alphitopolis and Basileios stoas were. If this is true the conventional topographical interpretations given by the excavators to the problem of the Basileios stoa (the first building mentioned by Pausanias as he entered the Agora in Kerameikos, see WT. 16) are no longer valid.

70. *Hesperia* 33, 1964, p. 225, No. 73 ca. middle of 2nd c. B.C.

vacat?

[. .]ης π[- - - -]

[. . .]ι[.]αι του[- - - -]

κα[ὶ] τάσδε προσ[μετρ - - - -]

vacat

ἐ[ν] Θησείο[υ στοᾶι]

ὁ τὸν σῖτον παρα[γγέλλων? - - -]

ὁ τὸν σῖτον πρι[άμενος? - - - -]

ὑπηρέτης ἐξα[γέτω - - - -]

καὶ τάσδε προ[σμετρ - - - -]

10　ὑπηρέτης ἐπ[ιστ - - - -]

vacat

and to (measure) those...
In (the Stoa) of Theseion.
The one ordering the grain - - - the one who bought the grain - - the (state) servant must take out - - and those are to be (measured) - - (and the state) servant (must inspect?) - -

This recently published inscription verifies our assumption above that the "stoa by the Basileios Stoa" or "Theseion" was connected with the grain trade. Even without my restorations which are based on the testimonia quoted above (TA. 68, 69), this valuable epigraphic source is the definite proof of the connection of the Theseion in the Agora in Kerameikos with the grain trade. The inscription appears to be a fragment from an official document giving information concerning the trade regulations for sellers and buyers of grain and the places of trade according to the laws of state control.

BREAD
(WT. p. 194; T. 636)

71. Archestratos (*Gastronomy*) in Athen. III. 112b.

.... τὸν δ' εἰς ἀγορὰν ποιεύμενον ἄρτον
αἱ κλειναὶ παρέχουσι βροτοῖς κάλλιστον ᾿Αθῆναι.

...*and the most excellent market-made bread which the renowned city of Athens provides to the mortals.*

From an archaeologist's point of view the great reputation of the Athenian "market-made" bread is more interesting than that of the simple "market bread" (cf. WT. 636) because it indicates that there were bakeries in the Agora area.

It seems that the bread sales were under state inspection and control as were the flour and grain sales (TA. 1, 68).

72. Kock, *Com. Att. Fragmenta*, p. 269 (1325) 5th c. B.C.

Μητίοχος μὲν γὰρ στρατηγεῖ, Μητίοχος δὲ τὰς ὁδούς,
Μητίοχος δ' ἄρτους ἐπωπᾷ, Μητίοχος δὲ τἄλφιτα,
Μητίοχος δὲ πάντ' ἀκεῖται, Μητίοχος δ' οἰμώξεται.

*Metiochos, you see, is general, Metiochos inspects the roads,
Metiochos inspects the bread, and Metiochos inspects the
flour,
Metiochos takes care of all things, Metiochos will come to
grief.*

The unknown poet of the old comedy, in ridiculing the many offices held by Metiochos, one of the "right hands" of Pericles, (cf. Plutarch, *Moralia*, 811f) mentions the inspection of bread as a particular office. More important is the fact that it is distinguished from the inspection of flour, indicating that the two were generally considered to be two separate offices.

OPSON
(WT. p. 194. T. 637)

73. Alexis, (*Plaidrias?*) in Athen. VII, 340b. ca. 372-270 B.C.

A. 'Αγορανομήσεις, ἂν θεοὶ θέλωσι σύ,
ἵνα Καλλιμέδοντ' εἰς τοὖψον, εἰ φιλεῖς τι με
παύσῃς καταιγίζοντα δι' ὅλης ἡμέρας
B. "Εργον τυράννων, οὐκ ἀγορανόμων λέγεις·
μάχιμος γὰρ ἀνήρ, χρήσιμος δὲ τῇ πόλει.

A. You shall be Aedile if the gods approve
So that you may stop Kallimedon descending
Like a whirlwind all day upon the fishmarket.
B. You speak of work for tyrants, not for Aediles
For the man is brave and useful to the city.

According to this fragment the Agoranomoi (Aediles) were the magistrates supervising the Opson as well as the rest of the marketplace.

74. Timocles, (*Epichairekakos*) Athen. VI 241a   4th c. B.C.

ἀγορὰν ἰδεῖν εὔοψον εὐποροῦντι μὲν
ἥδιστον, ἂν δ' ἀπορῇ τις ἀθλιώτατον.

...to see a market full of buys is a great joy for anyone
who has money; a great torture for those who have not.

75. Athenæus, XIII, 580c   2nd-3rd c. B.C.

Εἰς τὴν ἀγορὰν λέγουσιν αὐτὴν ἐξεῖναι
καὶ τοὖψον ἐφορᾶν καὶ πολυπραγμονεῖν πόσου
πωλεῖθ' ἕκαστον...............

They say that she came out to the market, inspected the
opson, and tried hard to learn the price of each thing..

Cf. WT. 649.

76. Ephippos. (*Philyra*) Athen., VIII, 358f-359a 4th c. B.C.

A .... παππία, βούλει δραμὼν
εἰς τὴν ἀγορὰν κᾆτ' ἀγοράσαι μοι, B. φράζε τί

A. ἰχθῦς φρονοῦντας, ὦ πάτερ, μὴ μοι θρέφη.
B. οὐκ οἶσθ' ὅτιὴ τἀργύριον ἐστ' ἰσάργυρον;

A. *Popsy, would you like to go to market*
And buy some fish for me? B. What shall I buy?
A. *Some grown up fish, my father, no small babies.*
B. *Do you not yet know the value of money?*

77. Ephippos, (*Oveliaphoroi*) Athen., VIII, 359a-c. 4th c. B.C.

A. .... ἀλλ' ἀγόρασον εὐτελῶς·
    ἅπαν γὰρ ἱκανόν ἐστι B. φράζε δέσποτα.

A. μὴ πολυτελῶς ἀλλὰ καθαρείως, ὅτι ἂν ἦι,
    ὁσίας ἔνεκ' ἀρκεῖ τευθίδια σηπίδια·
    κἂν κάραβός τις ἢ λαβεῖν, εἷς ἀρκέσει
    ἢ δύ' ἐπὶ τὴν τράπεζαν· ἐγχελύδια
    Θήβηθεν ἐνίοτ' ἔρχεται. τούτων λαβέ.

A. *But buy cheaply, for anything will do.*
B. *Just say how, Boss.*
A. *Don't be extravagant, though not mean or stingy;*
Whatever you buy will be enough.
Some squids and cuttle fish, and should there be
Some lobsters in the market, one should be fine
Though two look well on the table. Now some eels
Come in from Thebes sometimes. Get some of them.

78. Mnesimachos, (*Dyscolos or Oveliaphoroi*)
    Athen., VIII, 359 c-d   4th c. B.C.

    ....σύντεμνε καὶ
    ἐπεξαπάτα με. τοὺς μὲν ἰχθῦς μοι κάλει
    ἰχθύδι' ὄψον δ' ἂν λέγῃς ἕτερον κάλει
    ὀψάριον. ἥδιον γὰρ ἀπολοῦμαι πολύ.

...*be more brief and use diminutives. For fish say fishlings*
and if you want to say 'opson,' say 'opsarion.'' Thus I shall
be ruined in a pleasant way.

This fragment gives as a "nickname" of the Opson the word "Opsarion" from which comes the mediaeval and modern Greek ψάρι (fish).

MEAT
(WT. p. 196; T. 648-649)

79. Dioxippos, (*Historiographos*) Athen., III, 100e 4th c. B.C.

τὴν στοὰν διεξέπαιεν 'Αμφικλῆς μήτρας δύο
κρεμαμένας δείξας, ἐκεῖνον πέμπε, φησ', ἐὰν ἴδῃς.

Amphikles burst into the stoa, then showed two paunches hanging on a hook and said (to the seller), "Send me those two, if you can see them."

Amphicles selects the paunches that he wants to buy "in the stoa" where the meat on sale was hung up. Dioxippos was an Athenian comedian of the 4th c. B.C. and the scene of his comedy "The Historian" was undoubtedly set in Athens. (Cf. IG, II², 1622 (c54) where 'Αμφικλῆς 'Αλωπεκῆθεν, a rich Athenian is mentioned as trierarch. The second line more likely must be restored ἐκείνας instead of ἐκεῖνον.)

WINE AND VINEGAR
(WT. p. 199; T. 660-663)

80. Alexis in Athen., II, 67e   4th c. B.C.

....................................κοτύλας τέτταρας
ἀναγκάσας μεστὰς ἐμ' αὐτόθεν σπάσαι
ὄξους Δεκελεικοῦ δι'. ἀγορᾶς μέσης ἄγεις.

*You have compelled me to bring forth from there
Four half pint measurers of Dekeleian vinegar,
and now you drag me through
The middle of the market...*

This fragment reminds one of the location of the Dekeleian trade center known to be near the Stoa of the Herms near the center of the market or topographically not far from the

THE LATER AGORA IN KERAMEIKOS 93

Altar of the Twelve Gods. (cf. Lysias, XXIII, (Pankleon) 2-3. WT. 306)

TABLES
(WT. p. 192; T. 628-632)

81. Lysias, Fr. 50. in Pollux, X, 105

Μετ' ἀβακίου δὲ καὶ τραπεζίου πωλῶν ἑαυτόν.

Selling himself from a table with a "pricetag."

This sentence is used metaphorically, but it is the unique reliable mention of tables on which goods are out for sale. The fragment also gives the information that the sellers had the prices of their goods written on signs or tablets. (Cf. Athenaeus III, 117e, the question of a buyer to a seller in the dialogue of a fragment from the comedy Ἀπεγλαυκωμένος of Alexis "'Ἀβάκιον, ψῆφον· λέγε." The scene is in the Agora of Athens).

RIBANDS
(WT. p. 200; T. 665)

82. Eupolis, (*Prospaltioi*) Athen., VII, 326a   4th c. B.C.

μήτηρ τις αὐτῷ Θρᾷττα ταινιόπωλις ἦν,
ἐπὶ τῶν ὑφασμάτων λέγει καὶ τῶν ζωνῶν, αἷς αἱ γυναῖκες περιδέονται.

*His mother was a Thracian woman,
a seller of ribands;*

He means the woven textiles and the girdles with which women bind their waists.

PERFUME
(WT. pp. 202-203. T. 674-680)

83. Hypereides, *Against Athenogenes*, 12   ca. 350 B.C.

καὶ καταλαβόντες αὐτὸν πρὸς τοῖς μυροπωλείοις ἠρωτῶμεν
.... πολλῶν δ' ἀνθρώπων σ[υλλ]εγομένων καὶ ἐπακουόντων διὰ τὸ ἐν τῇ ἀγορᾷ τοὺς λόγους γίγνεσθαι,..........

We found him near the perfume shops and asked him...
and because a crowd had gathered and overheard our dis-
cussion as our altercation took place in the market...

84. Hypereides, *Against Athenogenes*, 14   330-324 B.C.

Ὁ μὲν τοίνυν εἷς νόμος κελεύ[ει] ἀψευδεῖν ἐν τῇ ἀγ[ορᾷ]....
σὺ [δὲ | ψε]υσάμενος [ἐν] μέσῃ τῇ ἀγορᾷ, συν[θήκα]ς
κατ᾽ ἐμ[οῦ ἔθ]ου.

Now the first law stipulates "No lying in the market"...
yet you lied in the middle of the market making a fraud-
ulent agreement with me...

85. Hypereides, *Against Athenogenes*, 19   330-324 B.C.

Οὗτ[ος] δὲ ὁ ἐκ τριγονίας [ὢν] μυροπώλης, καθ[ήμε]νος
δ᾽ ἐν τῇ ἀγο[ρᾷ] ὅσαι ἡμέραι, τρία [δὲ μυ]ροπώλια κεκτημέ-
νος, λόγους δὲ κατὰ μῆνα λαμβάνων, [οὐκ] ᾔδει τὰ χρέα·

Now this man, being a perfume seller following a family
tradition of three generations, sitting in the market day
by day, owning three perfume shops and getting monthly
reports from them, didn't know anything about the debts.

86. Athenæus, XV, 688 f.   2nd-3rd c. A.D.

(Τὸ μύρον) τὸ Παναθηναϊκὸν λεγόμενον ἐν Ἀθήναις.

The perfume called Panathenaic in Athens.

According to Apollonios in his treatise "On Perfume" a
special kind of perfume made in Athens was known as "Panathenaic."

87. Hypereides, *Against Athenogenes*, 6   330-324 B.C.

«Φορτία ἐστὶ τούτων ἐν τῷ ἐργαστηρίῳ, μύρον καὶ ἀλάβα-
στρον καὶ ζμύρνα».

"...and there are loads of sweet oil and alabaster (con-
tainers) and myrrh in the shop."

Thus we know that perfume was manufactured in the shops of the Agora.

88. Philemon, *Lithoglyphos.* Fr. 1   4th-3rd c. B.C.

πρὸς τῶι μυροπωλίωι γὰρ ἀνθρώπων τινῶν
ἤκουσα χαλκοῦν περιπατεῖν κλέπτην τινά·
ἄπειρος ὢν δὲ τοῦ λεγομένου πράγματο[ς]
'Αριστομήδην ἠρόμην παριόνθ' ὁρῶν.
ὁ δ' ἐνήλατ' εὐθύς μοι παραστὰς [τ]ῶι σκ[έ]λει
παίει τε λὰξ πύξ, ὥστε μ' ἐκθανεῖν· ἐπεὶ
μόλις γε φεύγων ἐξέπεσον ἄλληι λ[άθρ]α

(a) *I heard some fellows near the perfume-shop saying that a thief called. "Penny" was wandering about. As I didn't know what they were talking about, I asked Aristo-medes, whom I saw passing by. And he came straight up to me and jumped. at me, on my leg, and smote me with foot and fist—I nearly fainted to death; I ran away, and barely escaped. elsewhere in hiding...*

Aristomedes was an Athenian "marketplace character" as we know from the commentary of Didymos (col. IX, 52-60) on Demosthenes X, 70. The perfume shops in the Agora were apparently located in a spot very popular for the wandering crowds. The surname χαλκοῦς ("Penny") given to Aristo-medes describes him as a cheapskate and petty thief. The parallel also exists in modern Greek in the terms δεκαρολόγος and ἄνθρωπος τῆς δεκάρας.

BRONZEWORKERS

For the festival in honour of Athena and Hephaistos, see *Hephaistos.*

BARBERS

89. Plutarch, *De Garrul.*, c. 7, 505b   ca. 46-ca. 120 A.D.

Πρεσβυτῶν τινῶν ἐπὶ κουρείου διαλεγομένων ὡς οὐ φυλάτ-τεται τὸ Ἑπτάχαλκον καὶ κινδυνεύει τὸ ἄστυ κατ' ἐκεῖνο ληφθῆναι τὸ μέρος ἀκούσαντες οἱ κατάσκοποι πρὸς τὸν Σύλλαν ἐξήγγειλαν. Ὁ δὲ εὐθὺς τὴν δύναμιν προσαγαγὼν περὶ μέσας νύκτας εἰσήγαγε τὸ στράτευμα καὶ μικροῦ μὲν κατέσκαψε τὴν πόλιν, ἐνέπλησε δὲ φόνου καὶ νεκρῶν, ὥστε τὸν Κεραμεικὸν αἵματι ῥυῆναι.

"Hearing some old men conversing in a barbershop that the city was in danger of falling because Heptachalkon was not guarded, the spies carried the news to Sulla; he then immediately gathered his forces at this point and the same day, about midnight, succeeded with his soldiers in breaking into the city and almost razed it to the ground, spreading everywhere blood and dead bodies, so Kerameikos was flowing with blood."

That the barber shop was in the Agora is clear from this and the parallel narration of the same event, cf. TA. 69.

90. Plutarch, *Sulla*, 14, 1   ca. 46-ca. 120 A.D.

Ἐν δὲ τούτῳ λέγεται τινας ἐν Κεραμεικῷ πρεσβυτῶν ἀκούσαντας διαλεγομένων πρὸς ἀλλήλους καὶ κακιζόντων τὸν τύραννον, ὡς μὴ φυλάττοντα τοῦ τείχους τὴν περὶ τὸ Ἑπτάχαλκον ἔφοδον καὶ προσβολήν,... cf. 14, 4... Ὁ περὶ τὴν ἀγορὰν φόνος ἐπέσχε πάντα τὸν ἐντὸς τοῦ Διπύλου Κεραμεικόν.

"In the meantime they say, (Sulla's spies) heard some old men conversing in Kerameikos, blaming the tyrant for not having guards on the city wall near Heptachalkon. (cf. 14, 4. The blood which was shed in the market place covered all of the part of Kerameikos (which is inside the walled area) up to the Dipylon gates.

The information used by Plutarch in both accounts mentions the sack of Athens by Sulla in 86 B.C. and would seem to be based on the same historical source. The author, unknown to us, apparently meant that the information of the spies around the small gate of Heptachalkon was collected from the talks of citizens in one of the barbershops of the Agora.

COOKS

(WT. pp. 205-206)

91. Possidippos, (*Syntrophoi*) Fr. i   4th c. B.C.
(Athen., XIV, 695d)

A. ἐβάδιζες ἔξω τῶν πυλῶν μάγειρος ὤν,
B. ἐντὸς πυλῶν γὰρ μένων ἄν ἄδειπνος ἦν.
A. πότερ' οὖν ἀφεῖσαι; B. κατ' ἀγορὰν ἐργάζομαι
ἐπρίατο γάρ τις ὁμότεχνός με γνώριμος.

A. *Did you walk out of the gates being a cook?*
B. *If I stayed in, I would't have had any dinner.*
A. *Did they let you go free? B. No, I work in the market..*
Someone I knew who was also a cook bought me.

BANKERS

92. Lysias, IX, *For the Soldier*, 6   359-386 B.C.

Κἀμοὶ μὲν τὰ προειρειμένα διείλεκτο ἐπὶ τῇ Φιλίου τραπέζῃ.

And what I mentioned I said when I was at the bank of Philias.

Cf. *Strategion.* Most of the testimonia from other sources concerning bankers and money changers are collected on p. 192 of WT. and are considered to be "tables where goods are set up for sale."

93. Hypereides, *Against Athenogenes*, 9   ca. 350 B.C.

Ἐλθόντες δὲ ἐπὶ τὸ μυροπώλιον, τὸ μὲν γραμματεῖον τιθέμεθα παρὰ Λυσικλεῖ Λευκονοεῖ· τὰς δὲ τεττεράκοντα μνᾶς ἐγὼ καταβαλὼν τὴν ὠνὴν ἐποιησάμην.

Then we went to the perfumery; we deposited the doccument at Lysikles of Leuconoion and then I paid the forty minas and made the purchase.

This passage of Hypereides is a perfect description of "business" in a bank of the Agora, known by its owner's name, Lysikles from the deme of Leuconoion. The buyer and the seller went together to the bank of Lysikles and left there the signed document for the sale of the perfume shop. Then the buyer paid, through his bank account, the agreed amount of money (4000 Attic drachms). We know that prior to this the buyer had to deposit the forty minas in the bank. Cf. *Ag. Athen.* 5. "After I had collected from every source and had been a nuisance to my friends, I deposited the forty minas in the bank."

94. *Hesperia* 29, 1960, p. 51, No. 64 second half of 4th c. B.C.

[- - Πασ]ίων Π[ασικλέους (?) 'Αχαρνεὺς]
[- - παρ]ὰ Φορμίωνο[ς — — — — — —]
[- - διαιτητῶν δ' 'Α]θηναίων ὕσ[τερον - -]
[- - διαθήκ]ην τὴν [Πασίωνος — — — —]

- - *Pasion son of P(asikles? of Acharnae - -)*
- - *from Phormion - - (and when Athenian)*
arbitrators later - - the will of Pasion - -

The inscription restored above (cf. Demosthenes XLV, 17 for restoration of lines 3 and 4) is the only one to my knowledge mentioning banks and bankers in the Agora of the ancient city of Athens. It is a fragment from a stele of Hymeteian marble, broken on all sides, found on· April 18, 1935 in a context of late Roman date over the auditorium of the Odeion (M. 10).

The name "Phormion" in line 2 recalls immediately the famous banker of Athens, who is so well known from the speeches of Demosthenes. We know that Phormion succeeded the banker Pasion of Acharnae in the administration of the bank, married after Pasion's death his widow Archippe, and became the administrator of his estate as guardian of his sons Apollodoros and Pasikles.

From the literary sources the patronym of Pasion is not known, but we do know that he was a naturalized citizen (Demosth. XXXVI, 43), classified in the deme of Acharnai. Phormion, previously a freedman, became a citizen "in the archonship of Nikophemos" (361/0 B.C. - Demosth. XLI, 13), but we have no knowledge of either his patronym or his demotic.

In line 1 of the inscription the name of Pasion can be positively restored in connection with the mention of Phormion in line 2. The letter Π which follows the name Pasion is the first letter of the patronym which probably can be restored as Π[ασικλέους] from the name of his second son Pasikles (PA. 11654-Demosth., XLV, 84. XXXVI, 22). The demotic is well known from Demosthenes' speeches (PA. 11672) and its restoration is not subject to question.

The appearance of the names of Pasion and Phormion in a public document dated in the second half of the fourth century B.C. must be connected with the various lawsuits against Phormion, in which "Apollodoros son of Pasion of Acharnai" (PA. 1411) was concerned. The inscription clearly refers in line 3 to a decision "of the Athenians" connected perhaps with the bank of Pasion which had been transferred to Phormion. Further restoration is not assisted by the remains of line 4, but the inscription, although fragmentary, becomes very important for the archaeological search of the banking district in ancient Athens.

According to a passage in Demosthenes (XLV, 17), "after the death of Pasion the official arbitration of his will took place in the Poikile Stoa." It is possible that the text of the inscription in lines 3-4 refers to this document.

GOLDSMITHS, JEWELERS

95. Demosthenes, XXI, (*Against Meidias*), 22   347 B.C.

Παμμένης Παμμένους Θορίκιος ἔχω χρυσοχοεῖον ἐν τῇ ἀ-
γορᾷ, ἐν ᾧ καταγίγνομαι καὶ ἐργάζομαι τὴν χρυσοχοϊκὴν τέ-
χνην.

*I, Pammenes, son of Pammenes of Thorikos, have a gold-
smith's shop in the marketplace where I live myself and
also practice goldsmithery.*

For the correction of the demotic cf. SEG. XIV, 155.-REG.

Bull. Epigr. 1958, 209. The jeweler's inscribed gravestone was found not far from the Agora area and was brought to the Roman market where it still is. (Cf. "Polemon," V, 1952/3. pp. 145-146.)

KYPHON (TA. 17)

The Kyphon was a wooden structure where men (slaves, cf. IG, II², 380), were tied up to be whipped, It was probably identified with the "Podokakke" of the Solonian law which, as Lysias says, was called in his time "the Wooden Structure" (cf. Lysias, X, "Against Theomnestos," 16). The punishment was imposed by the Agoranomoi for bad behaviour in the Agora as well as by the Eleven for more serious crimes (Lysias, X,16). The Kyphon was in the Agora beside the building "where magistrates met," and the place was called "Kyphon" (cf. Aristotle, Aristophanes).

96. Lysias, X (*Theomnestos*), 16　　　　　384/383 B.C.

Καί μοι ἀνάγνωθι τούτους τοὺς νόμους τοὺς Σόλωνος τοὺς παλαιούς.

Νόμος. Δεδέσθαι δ' ἐν τῇ ποδοκάκκῃ ἡμέρας πέντε τὸν πόδα ἐὰν προστιμήσῃ ἡ ἡλιαία. Ἡ ποδοκάκκη τ' αὐτὸ ἐστὶν ὦ Θεόμνηστε, ὃ νῦν καλεῖται ἐν τῷ ξύλῳ δεδέσθαι.

And now read to me the old laws of Solon. Law: To be fastened in the pillory by the feet if the Heliaia so judges. This pillory, Theomnestus, is what we now call the stocks.

97. Demosthenes, XXIV (*Timokrates*), 105　　　353/2 B.C.

Δεδέσθαι δ' ἐν τῇ ποδοκάκκῃ τὸν πόδα πένθ' ἡμέρας καὶ νύκτας ἴσας ἐὰν προστιμήσῃ ἡ Ἡλιαία...............

To be fastened in the pillory by the feet for five equal days and nights if the Heliaia will so judge...

98. Aristotle, *Politics*, 5, 6　　　　　　4th c. B.C.

Δεθῆναι ἐν ἀγορᾶϊ ἐν τῷ κύφωνι.

To fasten him in the stocks in the marketplace.

99. Suidas, *Kyphon* 10th c. A.D.

Δεδέσθαι ἐν κύφωνι πρὸς τῷ ἀρχείῳ.

To be fastened in the stocks by the administration building.

100. Aristophanes, *Plutus*, 606 388 B.C.

εἴμι δὲ ποῖ γῆς; Ἐς τὸν κύφωνα.

Where on earth am I? In the stocks.

101. Schol. Aristophanes, *Plutus*, 606 388 B.C.

κύφων ὁ ξύλινος δεσμὸς ἐν ᾧ δεσμεύονται οἱ ἐν τῇ ἀγορᾷ, ὃν καὶ κυφῶνα περισπωμένως λέγουσι.

Kyphon: The wooden stocks where those in the market are fastened. There are some who pronounce the word putting the accent on the second syllable.

102. Kratinos, (*Nemesis*) [in Pollux, X. 177] 5th c. B.C.

ἐν τῷ κύφωνι τὸν αὐχένα ἔχειν.

Having the neck in the pillory.

103. Pollux, X, 177 2nd c. A.D.

ἢ που νοητέον ὡς σκεῦος ἦν ἀγορανομικόν, ᾧ τὸν αὐχένα ἐνθέντα ἔδει μαστιγοῦσθαι τὸν περὶ τὴν ἀγορὰν κακουργοῦντα.

(Commentery to TA 102): It must be understood that (pillory) was a structure of the Agoranomes in which those who misbehaved in the marketplace had to be fastened by the neck and get whipped.

104. Bekker, *Anectoda Graeca*, I. 228

Γραμματοκύφωνα: ἀντὶ τοῦ γραμματέα, ὅτι οἱ γραμματεῖς προσκεκυφότες γράφουσιν ἢ γραμματοκύφων οἷον ἐν ἀγορᾷ γραμματεὺς ἐπεὶ οἱ ἀγοραῖοι τῷ κύφωνι μαστιγοῦνται.

Gramatokyphona: Instead of scribe because the scribes lean over forward to write. Other Gramatokyphona: Like a scribe in the market place because the market rascals are whipped, fastened on the pillory.

105. IG. II², 380, lines 34-46   320/319 B.C.

[ἐὰν δέ τις] τούτων τί ποιεῖ ἐὰμ μ[ὲν δοῦλος, δεδέσθω καὶ λ]αμβανέτω Π πλὴ [ηγὰς ἐν τῷ κύφωνι αὖθις· ἐὰν δ'] [ἐλε]ύθερος οἱ ἀγορανόμοι Δ δραχμα]ῖς αὐτῷ, ἱε[ροποιοῖς ἀποδοσίμοις, ζημιούτ]ωσαν.

If someone does one (of the above prohibited things), if he is a slave he is to be fastened on the Kyphon and receive 50 lashes; if he is a free man the Agoranomoi must fine him 10 drachmas and this fine must be given to the hieropoioi.

For the restoration see "Platon," VIII, 1956, pp. 117-118.

106. Aristophanes, *Lysistrata*, 680   411 B.C.

Ἀλλὰ τούτων χρὴ πασῶν εἰς τετρημένον ξύλον ἐγκαθαρμόσαι λαβόντες τουτονὶ τὸν αὐχένα.

And they must fasten the necks of all those women in the holes of wooden pillories.

HONORARY STATUES
Introductory

107. Polyeuktus of Sphettos (*Against Demades*)   ca. 336 B.C.

Τί γάρ, φησί, σχῆμα ἕξει; Τὴν ἀσπίδα προβεβλήσεται· ἀλλὰ ταύτην γε ἀπέβαλεν ἐν τῇ μάχῃ τῇ περὶ τὴν Χαιρώνειαν, ἀλλὰ ἀκροστόλιον νεὼς ἕξει, ἔπειτα πυνθάνεται, Ποίας; ἢ τῆς τοῦ πατρός; ἀλλὰ βιβλίον· ἐν ᾧ φάσεις καὶ εἰσαγγελίαι ἔσονται γεγραμμέναι; Ἀλλὰ νὴ Δία στήσεται προσευχόμενος τοῖς θεοῖς; ἀλλὰ τοῖς ἐχθροῖς ὑπηρετῶν καὶ κακόνους ὢν τῇ πόλει καὶ τὰ ἐναντία πᾶσιν ὑμῖν εὐχόμενος;

And what will be the pose of this statue?
Is he going to stand holding a shield before him? But he threw away his shield in the battle of Chaironeia.

Or will he have the goosehead from a ship?... Of what ship?
Don't say the one of his father's (dinghy). Or will he hold
a book having a written record of convictions and
impeachments?
Or, by Zeus, could he even stand praying to the gods?
Who, the one who became the servant of the enemy and
bearer
of malice against the city, the one who wishes exactly the
opposite of what all of us wish?

Polyeuktus was attacking a decree proposed by Kephosodotus for Honors and an honorary statue to Demades in the Agora. The famous anti-Macedonian orator describes the types of honorary statues erected thus far in the Agora in a unique way and explains the reasons to the people of Athens for which any traditional type of honorary statue used as an original for the one of Demades would not be appropriate for his dishonest life.

The first examples of the ''statue with the shield'' were the statues of the general Chabrias (cf. Diodor. Sic., XV, 32, 5.-Polyainus, II, 1, 2.- Corn. Nepos, Chabrias, I, 2-3). The second type of statue referred to by the orator was that of the general *Konon* (known for the victorious seabattle of Knidus) and his son Timotheos (known for the seabattle of Leukas, and the cruise of Kerkyra.)

For the other two types we have no examples of statues erected before the year 336 B.C., but the statues of the orators and politicians, followed the type of statue ''Holding a book.'' Possibly the same type was also selected by Zeuxiades for the statue of Hypereides. For the last type of statues described as ''man praying to the gods,'' we know nothing, but Polyeuktus seems to have been describing statues well known to his audience.

108. IG. II², 4193, Lines 14-20   ca. 85/86-94/96 A.D.

καὶ χρυσοφο | ρίᾳ διὰ βίου τετειμημένον καὶ | ψηφίσματι
ἀναθέσεως ἀνδρι | άντων καὶ εἰκόνων ἐν παντὶ να | ῷ καὶ
ἐπισήμῳ τῆς πόλεως τό | πῳ.

honored also with the right to wear golden apparel
and by a decree giving him the right to dedicate
portrait statues and images in any temple and distinguished
site in the city for his lifetime.

The "standard type" of decree giving permission for the
erection of portrait statues "in every temple and remarkable
place in the city" must not be earlier than the time of Demetrius of Phaleron. This passage explains why more than
one statue base of the same person has been found in the
Agora area.

ALEXANDER

109. Hypereides, *Funeral Speech*, 21   322 B.C.

Φανερὸν δὲ ἐξ ὧν ἀναγκαζόμεθα καὶ νῦν ἔστι· θυσίας μὲν
ἀνθρώποις γ[ιγνο]μένας ἐφορᾶν, ἀγάλμ[ατα δὲ] καὶ βωμοὺς
καὶ ναοὺς [τοῖς μὲν] θεοῖς ἀμελῶς, τοῖς δ' ἀνθρώ[ποις] ἐπι-
μελῶς συντελούμενα, καὶ τοὺς <τού>των οἰκέτας, ὥσπερ ἥ-
ρωας τιμᾶν ἡμᾶς ἀναγκαζομένους.

Proof enough, for what I said are the things which we
are now pressed to practice: to observe sacrifices being
made to men, the preparation of cult-statues, altars and
temples neglected for the gods, but carefully perfected for
human beings, and to top it all, to be forced to honour
their servants as if they were heroes.

This clearly indicates that both Philip and Alexander were
deified before the Lamiac War and honored with statues,
altars and temples. Hypereides also mentions that the Athenians "were obliged" to honor "as heroes" the servants of
the Macedonian kings (Demades and others).

110. Hypereides, *Against Demosthenes*,   323 B.C.
      VIII, xxxii 2-5

ἐβουλέτ[ο ἐν ἀγορᾶι] | στῆσαι εἰκό[να Ἀλεξάν] | δρου
βασιλ[έως τρισκαιδε]κάτου θε[οῦ...

*...the one who wanted to convince (the citizens) to set
up a statue of King Alexander (in the market, as the)
thirteenth god.*

111. IG. II², 4260   2nd c. A.D.

['Ο Δῆμ]ος | [βασιλέα] 'Αλέξανδρον | [βασιλέως] Φιλίπ-
που υἱόν.

*The Assembly of the people (dedicated this statue of)
King Alexander, son of King Philip.*

Aetat imp. on a base found near Eleusinion.

CHABRIAS

112. IG. XIV, 1222   Aetat. Imper.

Χαβρ[ίας] | Κτησί[ππου] | Αἰξων[εύς].

Chabrias, son of Ktessippos of Aixone.

This inscription gives the demotic of Chabrias and not the
national "Athenian" as do all the other herms and statues of
famous authors and politicians made in Italy. So it is quite
possible that this herm was imported from Athens at an unknown date (cf. the commentary in "Polemon," V, 1952/3,
p. 143).

For the mention in Polyeuktus, see *Introductory.*

The meanings of the epigraphical and literary sources about
it recently caused the statue of Chabrias in the Athenian
Agora to become the subject of considerable discussion. Need-
less to say, none of the participants had any idea that the
principle clue (cf. TA. 107) to the understanding of the
statue's posture was to be found neither in Wycherley's compilation nor in the measurements of the alleged "monument"
which was ingeniously contrived by combining the inscribed
pieces of two statue bases, contemporary with each other, of
which only one was for the statue of Chabrias (cf. Eugene
Schweigert in *Hesperia* 9, 1940, pp. 314-320). The "monument" was created by means of a drawing and study by

Anne Pippin Burnett and Colin Edmondson published in
Hesperia 30, 1961, pp. 74-91. See also J. K. Anderson in *AJA*
67, 1964, pp. 411-413 for a good refutation of the mistaken
idea that the statue portrayed Chabrias "kneeling on one
knee."

In a statue base as yet unpublished, found along the Panathenaic Way near the Eleusineion, appears the inscription
ΧΑΒΡΙΟΥ in letters of the Imperial period. This is still
another element supporting the possibility that the herm of
Chabrias now in Rome was made in Athens during the same
period.

DEMADES

113. Hypereides, *Against Demades*, Fr. 79   ca. 336 B.C.

Περὶ οὗ πολλῷ ἂν δικαιότερον ἐν τοῖς ὀξυθυμίοις ἡ στήλη
σταθείη ἢ ἐν τοῖς ἡμετέροις ἱεροῖς.

This stele (with the decree honouring him) will be more
appropriate to be set up in the public latrines than in the
area of our temples and shrines.

The fragment mentions a stele which must have been erected
"in the area of our temples and shrines." The reference to
the Agora is clear enough because we know that the statue
of Demades was placed there (Deinarchus, I, 101), and the
stele mentioned might well have stood beside it.

114. Plutarch, *praec. gerendae reip.*, 820f. ca. 46-ca. 120 A.D,

Τῶν δὲ Δημητρίου τοῦ Φαληρέως τριακοσίων ἀνδριάντων
οὐδεὶς ἔσχε ἰὸν οὐδὲ πίνον, ἀλλὰ πάντες ἔτι ζῶντος προανηρέ-
θησαν· τοὺς δὲ Δημάδου κατεχώνευσαν εἰς ἀμίδας.

Of all those three hundred statues for Demetrius of
Phaleron, none obtained the patina of time, but all were
destroyed in his lifetime. As for those of Demades, they
melted them (and used the metal) for chamberpots.

The test mentions *statues* of Demades, who is here considered to be one of the tyrants of Athens. Cf. TA. 107, 109.

DEMETRIUS OF PHALERON

115. Diogenes Laertius, V, 77   3rd c. A.D.

Οὐ μὴν ἐκυρίευσαν τοῦ σώματος αὐτοῦ, ἀλλὰ τὸν ἰὸν ἀπέρυγον εἰς τὸν χαλκόν, κατασπάσαντες αὐτοῦ τὰς εἰκόνας καὶ τὰς μὲν ἀποδόμενοι, τὰς δὲ βυθίσαντες, τὰς δὲ κατακόψαντες εἰς ἀμίδας· λέγεται γὰρ καὶ τοῦτο, μία καὶ μόνη σώζεται ἐν Ἀκροπόλει.

They didn't capture his living body, but they let out their anger upon its bronze images, destroying completely his statues, some by melting, some by sinking, and some by cutting them apart into pieces which could be used as chamberpots, because even such a thing as this is said to have happened. So the one and only statue (of Demetrius) is saved on the Acropolis.

One of at least 300 statues of Demetrius (or more, cf. TA. 92) was in the Agora. As Diogenes Laertius says, the bronze from several of these statues was melted down to make chamberpots for the people. This happened before to the statues of Demades according to Plutarch who says the same thing happened to the statues of Demades as to Demetrius. The only known statue of Demades was in the Agora, and it is possible that the parallel mention of a statue of Demetrius in the same place existed in the text of the authors used as references by Plutarch. (cf. TA. 92).

DEMOSTHENES

116. *Oxyrrhynchi* Papyrus, 1800, Fr. 3. Lines 29-39 1st c. A.D.

Ἀθηναῖοι δὲ πά | [λι]ν τὴν ἐλευθερίαν ἃ | νακτησάμενοι ἐτίμη | σαν αὐτοῦ εἰκόνα χαλκ[ῆν] | ἀναστήσαντες ἐν Κερα | μικῶι ἐπίγραμμα τε | ἐν | στήληι ἐνεκόλαψαν το[ι] | ὁνδε «εἴπερ ἴσαν γνώμα[ι] ῥώμαν Δημόσθενες· ἔσχες, | οὔποτ' ἂν Ἑλλήνων ἦρξεν Ἄρης Μακεδών».

The Athenians, when they regained their freedom, honored him by setting up a bronze statue in Kerameikos and

*inscribing on a stele this epigram: "If you have had power
equal to your etc...."*

This fragment from an unknown biographer is interesting
for it indicates that the epigram was not on the statue's base
but on a stele and it gives a text in Doric dialect.

HYPEREIDES

117. IG. XIV, 1149-53   Aep. Imper.

Ὑπερίδης Ῥήτωρ
ΤΕΥΣΙΑΛΗΣ Ἐποίει (Ζευξιάδης)

*Hypereides the orator
Zeuxiades made it.*

This inscription was on a herm of Hypereides seen by
Visconti (Icongr. Gr. I, 272) in the Villa Mattei (in the area
of Rome), but it is now lost. The sculptor Zeuxiades was
one of the pupils of Silanion (Pliny, N. H., XXXIV, 8, 19).

118. Oxyrrhynchi Papyrus, 1800,Fr.8,ii,lines 30-32   1st c. A.D.

Ἀθη[ναῖοι δὲ πά | λ]ιν τὴν ἐλευθ[ερίαν ἀνακο] | μι-
σάμενοι χα[λκοῖς καὶ] αὐ[τ]ὸν ἀνδριᾶσιν ἐ[τίμησαν].

*The Athenians, when they regained their freedom, hon-
ored him by setting up bronze statues.*

This is the unique literary passage known which gives the
information that the Athenians honored Hypereides in the
same way as they did Demosthenes. It is not known who
proposed the decree for his honors, but is is a fact that
bronze *statues* were erected in Athens. Since Silanion is
known to have lived at the same time as Polyeuktus, the
sculptor of Demosthenes' statue and Zeuxiades, who, according to the herm's inscription, was the sculptor who made the
portrait statue which was copied in the Roman age, was a
student of Silanion, we may assume that Zeuxiades and Polyeuktus were contemporaries.

HYRKANOS

119. IG. II², 4700   1st c. A.D.

[- -] 'Υρκ[ανὸν - -]
[- - τ]οῦ Δή[μου καὶ τῶν]
[Χαρίτων - -] ΤΟΥΚΑ [- -]
['Επὶ ἱερείας δεῖνα Φ]ιλέου Φυλασίου θυ | γατρός |.

*- - Hyrk(anos) - - of the Demes and Charites - when
the priestess was - (- name -) - the daughter of Phileas of
Phyle.*

On a marble base found on the Acropolis. The text, according to my restoration is supported by Josephus (*Antiquitates
Judaicae*, XIV, 8, 5).

JUBA

A head from a statue found in the excavations of the
Greek Archaeological Society in the Stoa of Attalos has
been identified as Juba by Valerios Stais (N. M. 457, cf.
Papaspyridi, Guide..., p. 110).

JULIUS CAESAR

120. IG. II², 3222   48/47 A.D.

Ὁ Δῆμος | [Γ]άιον 'Ιούλιον Καίσ[αρα] | [ἀ]ρχιερέα
καὶ δικτά[τορα τὸν] | [ἑα]υτοῦ σωτῆρα κα[ὶ εὐεργέτην].

*The assembly of the People honors Gaius Julius Caesar
Pontifex Maximus and dictator, saviour and benefactor of
the Athenians.*

On a marble base of a bronze statue found in the north
tower of Panagia Pyrgiotissa.

L. FLAVIUS FLAMMA

121. IG. II², 3543   end of 1st c. A.D.

| Ὁ Δῆμος | | ὁ 'Αθηναίων τὸν | ἐπὶ τοὺς ὁπλείτας | στρα-
τηγὸν καὶ γυ | μνασίαρχον καὶ ἱε | ρέα Διὸς Βουλαίου | καὶ

'Αθηνᾶς Βουλαὶ | ας Λούκιον Φλάου | ῖον Φλάμμαν Κυδαθη |
ναιέα δικαιοσύνης καὶ | τῆς ἄλλης ἀρετῆς καὶ | τῶν εἰς τὴν
πατρίδα | φιλοτιμιῶν ἕνεκα.

*The Deme of the Athenians honors the general of the
heavy infantry and gymnasiarch and priest of Zeus Boulaios
and Athena Boulaia, Lucius Flamma of Kydathenaion for
his justice and other virtues and for his contributions to
the fatherland.*

Marble base of a statue found broken into four pieces in
Panagia Pyrgiotissa. W. uses it as T. 422, but without mention
in the chapter on honorary statues.

122. IG. II², 3544   end of 1st c. A.D.

Τὸν ἐπώνυμον | ἄρχοντα καὶ ἱερέ | α Δρούσου ὑπά | του
καὶ ἱερέα Διὸς Βουλαίου καὶ | 'Αθηνᾶς Βουλαί | [ας] Λού-
κιον Φλά | [ο] υιον Φλάμμαν | [ἀ] ρετῆς ἕνε [κεν] | [καὶ
| εὐνοί [ας· ἐπὶ] | [ἱερεί] ας Νη - - -.

*The archon eponymous and priest of Drusus the Superior
and priest of Zeus Boulaios and Athena Boulaia, Lucium
Flavium Flamma for good will and virtues. When the
priestess was Ne---.*

Marble base of another statue also found in Panagia Pyrgiotissa.

TIB. CLAUDIUS ATTICUS HERODES MARATHONIUS

123. IG. II², 3597, a-e   before 138 A.D.

Τὸν ἀρχιερέα τῶν Σεβαστῶν Τ. Κλαύδιον 'Αττικὸν 'Ηρώδην
Μαραθώνιον ἡ - - - ἰς φυλὴ ἀνέθηκεν εὐνοίας ἕνεκεν καὶ εὐ-
εργεσίας τῆς εἰς τὴν πατρίδα.

*The chief priest of the Emperors T (iberius) Claudius
Atticus of Marathon - - (name of phyle) - - dedicated for
his good will and good. deeds for the fatherland.*

PHOCION

124. Plutarch, *Phocion*, 38, I   ca. 46-ca. 120 A.D.

Καὶ μέντοι χρόνου βραχέος διαγενομένου καὶ τῶν πραγμάτων διδασκόντων οἷον ἐπιστάτην καὶ φύλακα σωφροσύνης καὶ
δικαιοσύνης ὁ δῆμος ἀπώλεσεν ἀνδριάντα μὲν αὐτοῦ χαλκοῦν
ἔστησαν, ἔθαψαν δὲ δημοσίοις τέλεσι τὰ ὀστᾶ.

*It was not long before the situation of their affairs
taught them how vigilant a magistrate and how excellent
a guardian of the virtues of justice and sobriety they had
lost. The people erected a bronze portrait statue (of Phocion) and buried his remains at public expense.*

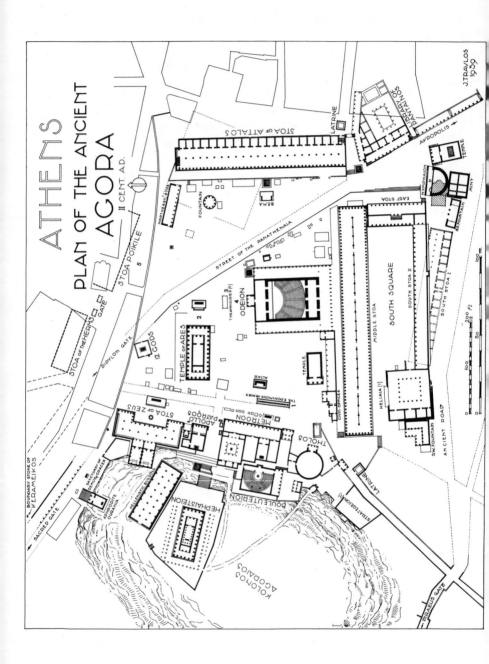

ATHENS
PLAN OF THE ANCIENT
AGORA
II CENT. A.D.

J. TRAVLOS 1939

STOA POIKILE   5

STOA OF THE HERMS   GATE

DIPYLON GATE

BOUNDARY STONE OF
KERAMEIKOS

SACRED GATE

STOA OF ZEUS

APOLLO PATROOS

12 GODS

TEMPLE OF ARES

2

3 TYRANNICIDES (?)
4 ODEION

Street of the Panathenaia

NORTHEAST STOA

FOUNTAIN

BEMA

STOA OF ATTALOS

LATRINE

LIBRARY OF PANTAINOS

AKROPOLIS

TEMPLE

NYMPHAION

MINT

SEPTFOUNTAIN

EAST STOA

TEMPLE

ALTAR

THE EPONYMOUS HEROES

METROON

BOULEUTERION

HEPHAISTEION

SANCTUARY OF
DEMOS & GRACES

HELLENISTIC BUILDING

APHRODITE OURANIA

THOLOS

STRATEGEION (?)

LATRINE

CIVIC OFFICES

HELIAIA (?)

MIDDLE STOA

SOUTH SQUARE

SOUTH STOA II

SOUTH STOA I

SW FOUNTAIN

ANCIENT ROAD

PRAIEUS GATE

KOLONOS AGORAIOS

100 m.

200 Ft.
0   50   100
0   100   200 Ft.

INDEX

Authors and Inscriptions

Reference is given to the two groups of testimonia here collected. Roman numerals (I-LIX) indicate testimonia referring to the Agora in the Old Town; Arabic num - bers (1-124) indicate testimonia referring to the later Agora in Kerameikos. The addition of n following a number indicates that mention of the text appears in the note or commentary of the text so designated.

INDEX

Modern Scholars

INDEX
Subjects

[The following subject references are to page numbers, rather than to testimonia. In the cases of gods, goddesses and heroes whose cults were interrelated, the phrase 'rel. to' is used rather than 'relation to cult of.']

Academy: mentioned in Strabo, 76

Aglauros: distinct from "Bride," 23,48; location of sanctuary of,29-30,48;the Ephebic oath in, xiii,48;rel.to cult of Nymphs,48; to Cecrops,48; to Demeter Chloe,14; to Kourotrophos, 9, 14: to Theseion, 29-30

Agoranomeion: 81

Agoranomoi :fines & punishments imposed by, 100-101; supervising the "opson," 90; see Kyphon

Agraulos (distinct from Aglauros): 48

Alexander of Macedon: 104-105;deification of,66-67,104-105;consequences of deification, 104; statue as 13th god in later Agora, 105; shrine in Kynosarges, 67; Alexander Herakles,67

Alphitopolis stoa: in later Agora,51,88; in Piraeus, 51

Aixone: 71

Altars: of Amphiaraos,55;of the Twelve Gods.70,93; of Zeus Meilichios,10-11: Eleos (Pity) see Zeus

Amphiaraos: intro.of cult in Athens, xiv; statue in later Agora,xiv;rel.to Asklepios,55; to Hygeia, 55

Anakeion: 29-30, 58-59

Aphidna: 71

Aphrodite "on Hippolytus":5-6,12

Aphrodite Pandemos:location of sanctuary of. xvi-xvii,1-7;old and new temples,5; cult statues,5;inscriptions,3-7.49; finds from cult, 7; Pausanias' visit,xiv: cult relations,1-14;rel. to "Bride,"16-18; to Eros,4;to Hippolytus,12; to Nike,4;to Peitho,5,8-9; to Zeus,37

Apollo Patroos:18-19,56;cult in the "old town,"18-19,56;cult in later Agora, 56: rel.to Creusa (Nymphe, "Bride") 24,56: to Ion,24

Apollo Pythios (cult in "old town"):15; rel. to Herakles,20; oracles of,18-19

Araphen: 71

Archinos (of Koile): 28

Archegetai (gods,heroes): 71

Archives: see Metroon

Ares: temple of, 66-67

Aristogeiton: see Harmodios and A.

Artemis Phosphoros:cult in Athens,56; dedicatory inscriptions,56;see Phosphoroi

Asklepios: xiii-xiv; sanctuary of,12,41; rel. to Amphiaraos, 55

Astynomeion: 81

Athena:15; basket bearer of,14;rel.to Aglauros,14; to Ge Kourotrophos,14 to Themis,13-14; A.Boulaia,110; A. Hephaistia, 66; A.Phratria,73;A.Polias, 67

Attalos: stoa of,vii,62,87

Banks: see Bankers

Bankers: b.of Philias by the Strategion, 97; b. of Lysikles by perfume shops, 97; b.transactions,97-98; b.of Pasion, 98,99; b.of Phormion, 98-99

Barbers: in later Agora, 95-96;talks in barbershops, 96

Basileios stoa: 51,88

Basket bearer: of Athena, 14

Blaute (Blaste, Balte): location of cult,39-42; sacred precinct, 39; inscriptions on, 39-40;"hero on blaute," 41-43;rel. to Aphrodite, 40; to Attic Zeus, 41; to Epimenides, 42-44; to Kourotrophos, 39-40

Bleachers: on s.slope of Acropolis, 2; in orchestra, 77-78; in Theatre of Dionysos, 77-78; on Panathenaic street,77

Booths: in later Agora, 85

Boule gate: 7

Boulaia, -os: see Athena B.,Hera B., Themis B., Zeus B.

Bouleuterion: in later Agora, 74; used by Boule of the 400, 74

Boundary markers: of Agora, xi; of Enneakrounos, 27-28,31; of Metroon on Museum Hill, 75; of sanctuary of the "Bride," 22; of Pelargikon, 21,22;of